MusicTech MAGAZINE
TEN MINUTE MASTERS

D1257253

PC Publishing

PC Publishing
Keeper's House
Merton
Thetford
Norfolk IP25 6QH
UK

Tel +44 (0)1953 889900
Fax +44 (0)1953 889901
email info@pc-publishing.com
website http://www.pc-publishing.com

First published 2006

ISBN 1 870775 04X

British Library Cataloguing in Publication Data
A catalogue record for this book is available from the British Library

Cover design by Hilary Norman Design Ltd

Printed and bound in Great Britain by Biddles, Kings Lynn, Norfolk

Contents

1   **Analogue synthesis** *1*

2   **Arranging rhythm** *5*

3   **Audio analysis** *9*

4   **Burning audio CDs** *13*

5   **Cabling** *18*

6   **Compression types** *23*

7   **Compressing audio** *27*

8   **Compression** *32*

9   **Copyright** *36*

10 **Delay** *40*

11 **Digital errors** *44*

12 **Digital audio** *48*

13 **Envelopes** *52*

14 **EQ** *56*

15 **Exciters** *60*

16 **Fades and crossfades** *64*

17 **Filters** *68*

18 **FireWire** *72*

19 **FM synthesis** *76*

20 **Granular synthesis** *80*

21 **Harmonics** *84*

22 **Microphones** *88*

23 **MIDI** *92*

24 **Mixers** *96*

25 **Oscillators** *100*

26 **Plug-ins** *104*

27 **Reverb** *108*

28 **Samplers** *112*

29 **Sequencers** *116*

30 **Stereo** *120*

31 **String synths and samplers** *124*

32 **Surround sound** *128*

33 **Synchronisation** *132*

34 **Time and pitch** *136*

35 **Vocoders** *140*

36 **Wireless** *144*

Index *148*

Analogue synthesis

Many forms of synthesis are now available to the musician, but it wasn't always so. It wasn't until the development of electronic circuitry that musicians had the most powerful creative force at their disposal. Arguably, the first 'electronic synthesizer' was the Theremin developed by Leon Theremin in the 1920s. During the next two decades there appeared various electronic organs and then the RCA Music Synthesizer.

A basic synthesizer patch using just the three main analogue modules – VCO, VCF and VCA.

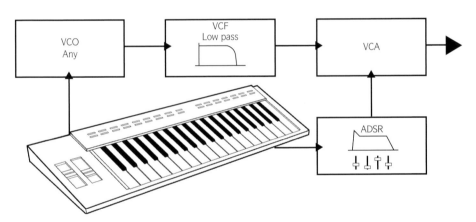

Several companies began developing synthesizer circuits although Robert Moog is commonly regarded as the father of synthesis, primarily through the development of voltage control. Moog synthesizers appeared commercially in 1964 and the rest, as they say, is history.

Hardwired

Most early analogue synths, Moogs in particular, were modular in nature. That is, you got a set of synth modules that you had to patch together yourself in order to make a sound. It's a very flexible system, but it means you need to know a bit about synthesis before you can even get the thing to squeak.

Many modules ended up being connected in the same way, so a natural development was to produce an instrument with the common routings preset or hardwired. This traded some flexibility for ease of use, but it proved a popular move and most synths, particularly those with a keyboard designed for performance, soon had a degree of hardwiring in them.

Why analogue?

Technology has moved on apace since the 1960s. We now have reliable and powerful digital circuitry plus, with modern computers, the ability to emulate synth circuitry in software. Even though there are no voltages, as such, in soft synths, many adopt a pseudo CV system. These include Arturia's Moog Modular V and Propellerhead's Reason, among others. Even modern hardware synths – which are, of course, built with digital circuitry – interface with the user through analogue-type controls. And there are still companies such as Analogue Systems (www.analoguesystems.co.uk) and Doepfer (www.doepfer.de) that produce genuine analogue synth modules.

Why? Well, the reasons are three-fold. First of all, the principles of analogue synthesis are easy to understand and fairly intuitive. If you understand the basics, it's fairly easy to get acquainted with any synth – far easier than having to learn a new form of synthesis. However, even alternative forms of synthesis use building blocks from analogue synthesis such as envelope generators and filters.

Propellerhead's Reason is a rack containing synth modules you can link together with virtual patch cords.

Secondly, there is something very appealing about twiddling dials and moving sliders – these things are fun to work with. Soft synths aren't so hands-on, but they're still fun, usually many times more powerful than hardware instruments and much, much cheaper.

Finally, many old analogue synthesizers had a distinctive sound – the Moogs were famous for their 'fat' sound, a result of the filters used in their construction. Devotees claim this character is not found in digital synths, and many software developers have worked hard to emulate vintage synth circuitry in software.

So can a soft synth or a hardware synth that uses digital circuitry genuinely be called analogue? Strictly speaking, analogue synthesizers are those created with analogue (as opposed to digital) circuitry. The first synthesizers were analogue because, well, digital circuits had not been invented. However, the term has expanded to include almost any synth that behaves in an analogue fashion.

How's it done?

The analogue synthesis approach to creating sound is pretty simple. It uses three main building blocks – tone generation, tone shaping and volume shaping. In other words, you take a waveform produced by an oscillator, use a filter to change the tone, and shape the volume with an envelope.

Linking modules together is fine, but you need a way to control them and to play specific pitches, rather than having to twiddle a dial every time you want a new sound. The big breakthrough came with Moog's development of voltage control. This revolutionised analogue synthesizers and led to the development of modules such as the VCO (Voltage Controlled Oscillator), VCF (Voltage Controlled Filter) and VCA (Voltage Controlled Amplifier).

The pitch of a VCO was determined by voltages from a keyboard. The cutoff frequency of a VCF could be controlled by voltages from other modules. And the ADSR envelope generated voltages to control the VCA. The CV (Control Voltage) system enabled the output of any module to be patched to the input of any other – an incredibly powerful and versatile system.

If there was a downside it was the lack of standardisation. And this had nothing to do with the CV principle, but the way in which it was implemented. In true music industry style, different manufacturers used different voltage systems, so it was difficult to connect one company's synthesizer to another's, but eventually a one-volt-per-octave system came to dominate.

Gates and triggers

To control pitch, each key on a keyboard generates a voltage – the higher the key, the higher the voltage and the higher the pitch. In addition, a synth keyboard generates two other signals – a gate pulse and a trigger signal. The gate pulse lasts as long as a key is held down, telling the synth when a key is pressed and when it's released. This controls the envelope generator – the Attack phase begins when a key is pressed and the gate pulse starts, and the Release phase begins when the key is released and the gate pulse ends.

Some instruments, particularly modular systems, also have a trigger signal. This is simply an on/off signal, a short blip, that's generated as soon as a key is pressed, even if one is already being held down. It can be sent to the VCO to generate a new pitch, but without triggering a new envelope, enabling the player to create a slur.

Gates and triggers are not normally a feature of hardwired instruments as their functions are incorporated into the design.

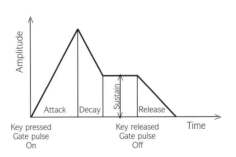

The Gate pulse generated by a keyboard determines when the ADSR generator triggers.

Analogue essentials

As well as the VCO, VCF and VCA, there are several other core analogue synthesis modules. These are discussed below:

- *LFO* The Low Frequency Oscillator is undoubtedly the most common additional module. Its low frequency oscillations can be applied in moderation to the VCO, VCF and VCA to add musical nuances such as vibrato and tremolo, or in excess to produce sirens and sounds that change tone over a long period of time. You can, in fact, build a very usable synth from just these four modules – VCO, VCF, VCA and LFO.
- *Sub-oscillator/Frequency Divider* Sub-oscillators were popular in early hardwired synths. They added another oscillator to the output, usually an

Tech terms

Vibrato
A variation in pitch produced by applying an LFO to the VCO.

Tremolo
A variation in amplitude produced by applying an LFO to the VCA.

Slur
The generation of a new pitch without triggering the ADSR envelope.

Frequency divider
A module that divides the source frequency by two, four, eight or some other amount. This can be used as a sub-oscillator or to generate rhythmic trigger pulses to control other modules.

Subtractive synthesis
A type of synthesis, like analogue synthesis, that starts with a harmonically rich sound source such as a square wave, and then removes harmonics by filtering.

octave or two below the original oscillator, to thicken the sound. More modern multi-oscillator synths can use a 'normal' oscillator, so dedicated sub-oscillators became less important. However, some modular synths have a Frequency Divider that can be used as a sub-oscillator, but which have many more uses such as creating pulses to trigger other sounds, effects or a sequencer.

- *Ring Modulator* This has two inputs and one output. The output is a combination of the sum and difference of the two input frequencies. Without doing any hard sums, this usually produces frequencies that 'inbetween' the notes in our Western scale. It's most commonly used to create 'metallic' sounds.
- *Glide/Portamento/Slew Limiter* Hardware synths have Glide or Portamento controls. Modular synths have a Slew Limiter. Their purpose is the same – to slide a note from one pitch to another, much the same effect as sliding your finger up a guitar string. Keyboard players cannot produce this effect naturally because each key produces a distinct semitone pitch. This module gives them 'slide-ability'.
- *Sample & Hold* As its name suggests, this samples the input signal and holds it until it's told to take another reading. Let's say you plug a sawtooth into the input and use a square wave for the trigger – when the square wave moves to the top of its cycle it triggers a new sample. Assume the square cycle is four times longer than the sawtooth cycle. Each time the S&H generator is triggered, the sawtooth wave will be a little higher in its cycle, so if you fed this into a VCO, you'd get four rising pitches. Slow down the square wave and you'd get more pitches in the series. If the two waveforms are not in sync or if you apply a random waveform such as noise to the input, then the output will be unpredictable. Plug this into a VCO for a random series of notes or apply to a filter for a random series of tone changes.

We've looked at the key principles behind analogue synthesis and some of the core modules used in analogue synthesizers. Not only will these help you to understand and use any analogue synthesizer, but they will also be useful when you come to use other forms of synthesis, too.

Further info

The very best primer on sound and synthesis is no longer available, but no apologies for mentioning it. Beg borrow or steal a copy of *A Foundation For Electronic Music*, published by Roland Corporation, one of a four-book set called The Synthesizer, designed for users of Roland's 100M modular synthesizer.

There are thousands of references on the web. Start by taking a look at these

www.geocities.com/roland_rock/analog.htm
www.fortunecity.com/emachines/e11/86/synth3.html
www.synthesizers.com
http://code404.com/faq

Arranging rhythm

The rhythm section is best described as the instruments which normally drive the rhythmic aspect of any composition or song. As such, they play a pivotal role in just about every contemporary composition in one way or another, particularly in dance music.

Traditional rhythm sections would have comprised drums, bass, guitar and piano, but with the advent of electronic instruments, this collection has expanded to include keyboards and synths. Although the sounds may have changed from the original construct, the methodology behind the way these instruments work together is largely unchanged.

Rhythm sections first distinguished themselves in jazz and big bands, with their primary role being the driving force behind the lead instruments. In the case of a big band, this would have meant backing anything up to 21 horn players. With that kind of force of numbers to contend with, it's hardly surprising that rhythm sections became the musical engine for most groups, playing hard in order to be heard above the rest of the band.

In a contemporary setting, little has changed, and it's no surprise that the kick or bass drum in most dance tracks maintains a '4-to-the-floor' feel in order to hammer home the beat.

An example of a basic drum groove. Notice the 4-to-the-floor kick part notated on the bottom line of the stave.

A more elaborate version of a basic drum groove. The kick and hi-hat parts are more embellished.

Instrumentation

The drum kit is the backbone of any rhythm section. It consists of three basic elements which provide the mainstay of any groove: the bass drum (or kick), snare drum and hi-hats. In one self-contained unit, it provides everything needed to power a song along: kick to provide a solid foundation to the time signature, snare to break up each bar on the second and fourth beats, and the hi-hat to sub-divide the beat further into 8th or 16th notes.

Other elements within the kit include cymbals and toms, but these are generally used for embellishment or to indicate a change in the song structure.

Before the advent of the electric bass, the bass part would traditionally have been played on an upright double bass. Today, we have many synths, both hardware and software, which can also provide this component for us. One popular option is Trilogy, from Spectrasonics, an all-in-one package that can realistically re-create upright, electric or synth basses.

Guitars and keyboards share a very similar role within a rhythm section. In 70s-derived funk, the guitar is crucial, providing chordal elements which drive forward in 8th- and 16th-note divisions.

Keyboards often provide a similar role rhythmically, particularly after the advent of the Hohner Clavinet or Fender Rhodes. In a more contemporary setting, many guitar parts have been replaced by synth sounds, which work in a very similar way.

By arrangement

When starting an arrangement, it's often a good idea to put your drums and bass in first. Given the wealth of good-quality sample CDs on the market these days, you may choose to use a loop. Alternatively, you may choose to program your own parts or mix-and-match with existing loops. In either case, make sure that the groove you are aiming for is achievable with the loop you are using. If you're programming your drum track, keep the individual elements of the kit on separate tracks, as it will make it easier to adjust the arrangement should you decide to change it later.

Once the drums are in place, move on to the bass part, but before laying anything down, consider the range that the instrument will play across. Bass sounds can appear very strong in one register of the keyboard, but really lose impact in another, so it's worth thinking about the line you want to play, working out the lowest note of the phrase and making sure that it doesn't sound weak in that register.

In addition to this, try to match some elements of your bass line to the kick drum that you have already laid down. Bass lines have far more impact if the notes you want to emphasise within a phrase are matched to a beat on the kick drum. The obvious choice is the first beat of the phrase, but that's not always the most appropriate. Consider Prince's Alphabet Street: there is a rest on the first beat of every other bar. It initially sounds a little strange, but it's highly innovative and it works. On the other hand, think of Good Times by Chic, in which the very distinctive and relentless bass pattern is tracked by a kick pattern which backs it up – possibly the finest example of a definitive bass line.

The shape of space

Once your drum and bass elements are taking shape, it's time to add keyboards or guitar. If you want to use both instruments, it is often a good idea to leave a little space between the respective parts for one to interplay with the other. You could explore the question-and-answer device, whereby the guitar plays a line which is subsequently 'answered' by a keyboard chord or riff.

Alternatively, the guitar could follow the rhythm of the track – much the same as the hi-hat – while the keyboard plays sustained chords. One of the best examples of this sort of interplay can be found on the Scritti Politti album Provision; producer/programmer Dave Gamson uses an extensive array of

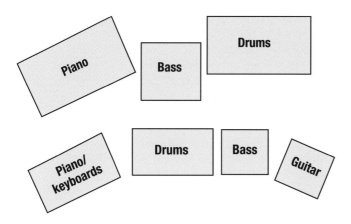

timbres which blend together to form a wonderful tapestry of sound.

Arranging the mix

Having thought about the notes the various instruments will play, it's now time to consider where to place those instruments in your mix. A basic concept to bear in mind when mixing is that the lower-frequency instruments should be panned centrally in the mix. This is not a hard-and-fast rule, but it works effectively in the majority of situations.

It is a good idea to think about the way the instruments you have used will sound in a live environment – not at Wembley Stadium, where there will be monitoring wedges and top-quality gear, but at your local pub, with only average facilities.

Ensure the kick drum and the bass are panned dead centre and work on mixing these two instruments first. The bass will probably require a little compression to give a good foundation to the mix. One by one, add the other percussive elements until the entire kit is in place. The snare often tends to sit in the middle of the mix, too, while hi-hats sound best when panned to one side (which side you choose is a matter of personal preference).

If you have a guitar part, balance out the hi-hat by placing it on the opposite side. Too much rhythm on one side of the mix won't give the impression of space that you probably want. By the same token, the keyboard will probably be less rhythmic, so offset that against the guitar part so that they are on opposite sides.

The final mixdown

Mixing is a good example of a task that requires an objective, focused approach. As you become more skilled at arranging and mixing a rhythm section, you should find that you begin to get a solid, tight sound, with an element of space between the various instruments and phrases.

You can pick up many tricks and techniques from listening closely to the type of music you want to make. Initially, you will have to train your ear to isolate the various parts in an overall mix, but it becomes easier with practice. There is much to learn from past masters; listen to as wide a range of music as you can to broaden your appreciation of different approaches.

Above all, be brave and experiment. As long as you keep copies of your

Tech terms

Rhythm section
Collective name for the instruments that comprise the driving force behind a band: drums, bass, guitar, keyboards and percussion.

Arranging
The process of distributing the chords and melody of a song across a set of instruments. This is sometimes known as orchestration, although this is linked more with classical music.

4-to-the-floor
A term often used by drummers to refer to the kick/bass drum playing on every beat of the bar.

Drum score
A drum part notated on a standard musical stave. The kick is positioned on the bottom line, snare on the middle line and the hi-hat on the top line.

Further info

Books
Arranging Music For The Real World, Vince Corozine
Basic Concepts Of Arranging And Orchestrating Music, Tom Bruner
Arranging In The Digital World, Corey Allen

Software
Trilogy Total Bass Module, Spectrasonics www.spectrasonics.net

Listening
Lovesexy, Prince
Good Times, Chic
Provision, Scritti Politti

Audio analysis

Given the amount of time we all spend working with sound, it's amazing to think how little we directly know about the medium we're working with. The truth is, we've all become accustomed to using our ears and brain to analyse and interpret the complex set of vibrations that sound is. In many situations, however, engineers will often call upon more scientific means of analysing a sound's attributes, to better rationalise their application of EQ, compression, effects and so on. But how do these different audio analysers work, and what information can we feasibly extract from them?

Metering is one form of analysis that's commonly used to better understand the behaviour of an audio signal. Although incredibly important for establishing good recording levels, metering gives feedback on only one of the many components of sound that can be visually represented – that of time-based amplitude fluctuations. But are these fluctuations all that our ears perceive? What about other components, such as pitch and timbre – aren't these qualities just as important (if not more so) than a sound's given amplitude at any point in time? By moving from time-domain analysis to more complex frequency-domain analysis, we can extract far more information about the individual components of a sound and how our ears perceive it.

The two domains

When we're recording, we largely visualise sound in the time domain – either via the meters attached to consoles and recorders, or the waveform displays used for audio editing. To move beyond the time domain, however, we first need to review some fundamentals of sound and the perception of timbre. Joseph Fourier – a French mathematician who performed some groundbreaking work into audio analysis – explained that sound or timbre could be broken up into its constituent components based on its fundamental frequency and a series of harmonics. So, as we now widely accept, a square wave can be broken down into a series of sine waves – in this case, the fundamental and a series of odd harmonics.

The techniques developed by Fourier, called Fourier Analysis, used complex mathematical formulae to decode a time-domain amplitude plot (as produced by an oscilloscope) into a frequency-domain spectrum plot; this illustrated the relative positioning and amplitude of the fundamental and the harmonics. The resulting spectrum plot provides far more information, giving the user a better understanding of the pitch and timbre of the signal in a way that

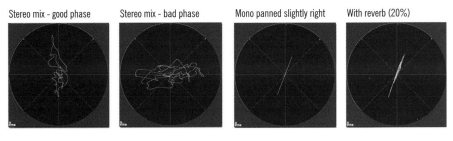

Stereo mix - good phase   Stereo mix - bad phase   Mono panned slightly right   With reverb (20%)

Characteristic plots from a Lissajous phase scope, illustrating how both phase and stereo information can be read.

was (as Fourier himself argued) much closer to how our ears perceive and decode sound. Put simply, an FFT (or Fast Fourier Transform) plot ideally visualises our perception of sound and music.

Graphs and waterfalls

Nowadays, of course, the complex calculations necessary for FFT analysis can be carried out in real time by a relatively modest computer. Once FFT analysis has been performed, there are a number of ways the resulting data can be displayed and handled, including spectrographs, spectrograms and waterfall displays.

One of the main reasons for the variety of display formats lies in how an FFT plot deals with the thorny issue of time. By existing in the frequency domain rather than the time domain, an FFT plot is only a snapshot of a given period. To add time back into the equation, a series of snapshots are taken (as with digital recording) and placed one after another to illustrate how the sound changes throughout its duration.

The most basic of FFT displays is the spectrograph, which plots the frequency response. Usefully, many software equalizers (such as Logic Pro 7's channel EQ) are now starting to support real-time spectrographs as a means of visualising a sound and its associated harmonics when applying EQ – finally an EQ curve can directly equate to something meaningful! In mastering, for example, a spectrograph can also function as a means of quantifying bass and treble rolloff on a track – a task that is difficult to achieve with tired ears in unfamiliar listening environments. As with all FFT displays, the sample size of the spectrograph will have a direct correlation with the detail of its output, so a plot size of 2,048 points will produce a more informative output than one with 512 points.

FFT waterfalls further the concept of spectrographs: rather than the windows being drawn over the top of one another, they are are ordered sequentially on a 3D 'waterfall' axis. This method gives a far better visualisation of what is taking place over time, producing a landscaped view of the subject sound. A good example of a waterfall is the IR display found in Altiverb 5 – here you can see both the duration and timbral qualities of the reverb tail, so that bright reverbs look and sound dense in harmonics.

Sound in colour

The ultimate tool for FFT analysis has to be the spectrogram/sonogram, which provides a unique and readable fingerprint of the sound being analysed. The spectrogram is similar to the waterfall concept, but viewed directly from above, with time on the horizontal axis, pitch on the vertical axis and ampli-

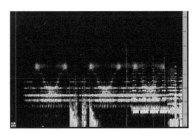

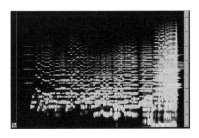

The left hand spectrogram output is from Peter Gabriel's Long Walk Home. The piece is largely sound design-driven – notice the long drones and sweeping sounds, with more harmonic components appearing later. The two blips are bass drums.

On the right is John Williams' score for Star Wars Episode III. The piece starts with high strings (note the harmonics at the start), with a gentle, thematic and chordal development, crescendoing approximately one minute into the piece.

tude expressed as shades of colour. The spectrogram works well because of the variety of information you can extract from it, although they can take some time to fully get to grips with.

Obviously, some aspects of the harmonic structure can be decoded quite easily, but other qualities – such as dynamics, levels of ambience, compression and transients – can all be read from this powerful method of audio analysis.

Take a close look at a typical spectrogram and you should be able to identify melodies, bass lines and chords within the overall texture. Look further up and you'll spot the trace harmonics echoing the patterns of the original parts (the lines should appear thinner and darker), or clusters of noise and formants in the 8–16kHz range. With their sharp transients and broad sound spectrum, drums appear as straight vertical lines; if the music is tight and well mixed, the lines should be clear and well pronounced. Dynamic range should also be evident, either across time (ideally, the subject track should get louder and quieter) or with respect to loud and quiet sounds in the mix (these appear distant and blue).

Lissajous vibrations

Returning to the time-domain analysis, another important tool is the Lissajous phase scope. The principles date back to the work of physicist Jules-Antoine Lissajous, who was intrigued by the visualisation of vibrations and how two different frequencies interacted with one another. The Lissajous phase scope works by combining the left- and right-hand signals on the X and Y axes of an oscilloscope. As well as being fascinating to look at, the Lissajous

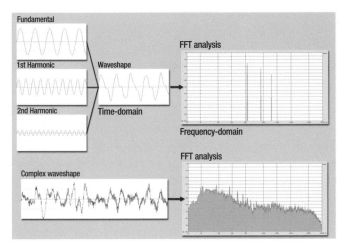

FFT analysis enables a waveshape to be plotted in its original harmonic structure. The top example shows the derivation of the waveform and the resulting FFT plot, while the bottom example illustrates an FFT output on more complex material.

Tech terms

Time domain

Time domain is a term used to describe how a signal fluctuates over time. In the case of audio analysis, time domain corresponds to the vibration and amplitude of a given audio signal.

Frequency domain

Frequency domain illustrates how a given signal sits within a range of frequency bands (usually between 20Hz and 20kHz). With frequency-domain analysis, time is completely variable, with the sample window lasting for an infinite amount of time.

Middle and side

Rather than expressing a stereo signal as distinct left/right components, an alternative approach is to use middle and side metering. Here, the signal is visualised by its shared components (the middle) and the differences between left and right (the side).

phase scope provides one of the best ways of quantifying the 'stereoness' of a given signal and the respective balance between the middle and side components of a signal.

Like the spectrogram, a Lissajous phase scope takes a little time to fully understand, but can be vital when dealing with phase problems or mixing and mastering. In-phase mono signals appear as a single straight line. If the signal is panned, the angle of the line changes to the left and right axis accordingly. Add further signals and the Lissajous phase scope begins to emit its characteristic geometric shapes, with wider patterns indicating a greater amount of left/right orientation, and thus a wider stereo image. In cases where phase becomes problematic, the orientation of the output becomes increasingly horizontal, as opposed to the phase-perfect vertical.

Visual stimuli

Gaining a more informed understanding of the visualisation of sound can only be beneficial to the process of writing and recording music. What's intriguing is just how beautiful a good recording or piece of music can appear to the eye – look for clearly identifiable layers of sound that change and develop in interesting ways, confirming what our ears may well have known for a long time.

More importantly, however, as the number of ways we are able to look at sound increases, the closer we become to experiencing sound as a tangible entity, rather than just vibrations in the air.

Further info

For a fascinating insight into sonograms and mastering practices, visit
www.airwindows.com/analysis/Dynamics.html
For more information on Joseph Fourier and FFT, visit
mathworld.wolfram.com/FastFourierTransform.html
www-gap.dcs.st-and.ac.uk/~history/Mathematicians/Fourier.html
Sound engineering isn't always about music: this site explains some of the techniques used in Forensic Audio Analysis
caeaudio.com/forensicaudio.html
If you're interested in sound analysis software (some of it freeware), visit
www.channld.com/mts.html
ems.music.uiuc.edu/beaucham/software/armadillo/
www.soundhack.com/freeware.php
www.mhlabs.com/metric_halo/products/foo/

Burning audio CDs

Creating an audio CD can be as simple or as involved as you want to make it. With most CD-R software you drag audio files into a playlist, click the Burn button, go and have a cup of coffee and come back to an audio CD. And that's fine. However, there's more to creating an audio CD than that.

Brought to Book

When the CD format was being developed, it was seen as the answer to many data storage problems, each with their own requirements. Consequently there emerged a rather long list of CD formats named 'Books' to cater for each requirement. This is a list of just a few of those formats:

- *Red* This is the standard audio CD, recorded at 44.1kHz and 16-bit resolution.
- *Yellow* A general format for storing computer data and for multimedia use for playing audio and video from the CD.
- *Blue Enhanced CD*, also known as CD Extra, comprising audio and data sections and enabling the CD to be played on an audio player and in a computer.
- *White* Essentially video CD.
- *Orange* Defines the recordable CD format comprising CD-R, CD-RW and CD-MO with multi-session capability.

The main book of interest to musicians is the Red Book. Other formats can be created by general purpose CD-R software, but you really need dedicated audio CD software to take full advantage of the special audio CD features.
If you want to produce a 'normal' audio CD without any frills, then the utility that came with your CD-R drive will probably do the job. The two most popular bundled applications are Adaptec's Easy CD Creator and Ahead's Nero. Both of these are very easy to use, essentially involving little more than dragging audio files and dropping them into a playlist.

All at once

There are two ways a CD can be burned – disc at once (DAO) and track at once (TAO). As the names suggest, DAO burns the entire disc in one go, whereas TAO burns the disc a track at a time.

The problem with TAO is that the process records two run-out blocks at the end of a track, a link block and four run-in blocks at the start of the next

Ahead's Nero uses a drag and drop approach to creating audio CDs.

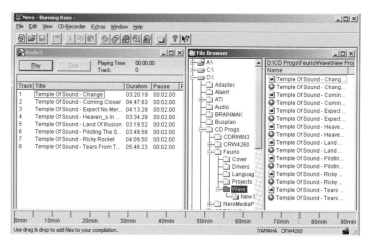

track. These are just 'housekeeping' data but they can confuse some dedicated audio CD players, which may click as they try to play them. CD-ROM drives don't have this problem because they don't read between the tracks. In addition, features such as changing the gap between tracks require DAO writing. The bottom line is simply to use only DAO when creating audio CDs. This is not a problem with modern CD-R drives but some older drives may not support DAO writing.

Nero's overburn section lets you set the maximum length of the CD, amid dire warnings of disaster should your system not be able to cope!

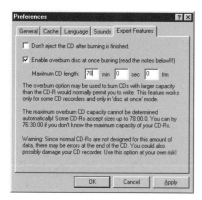

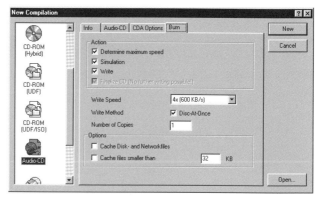

Nero has many disc-burning options. Of particular interest to audio CD creators is the DAO check box.

Good sessions

When CDs were first launched, one heavily promoted advantage was their massive storage capacity. Back then, however, not many people created 650MB of data in one go, so they could fill up a CD incrementally by writing to it in several sessions. This multi-session capability was probably most used with photo CDs where people were encouraged to put their photos on CD in several goes and then take them along to the chemist for printing.

A CD-R must be multi-session-compatible in order to read a multi-session CD – all modern ones are – but, again, this is not recommended for creating audio CDs.

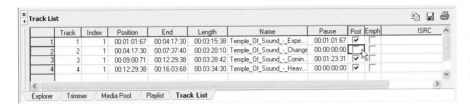

In CD Architect's Track List window you can alter any track's timings, set Protect flags and Emphasis flags, and even enter an ISRC code if you wish.

Write again

Another development to help users get the most from CDs is CD-RW. You can't write to a normal CD more than once because the writing process uses a laser to burn pits into the CD surface. CD-RW, however, uses a different material and the laser changes its state from crystalline to amorphous, enabling it to be written to many times. However, the reflectivity from CD-RW is not as great as standard CDs, and some players (including some computer-based CD drives) aren't able to read them. Drives need to be specifically CD-RW compatible. It's also unlikely that audio CD players will be able to read them. Needless to say, you need a CD-RW drive in order to write them.

CD-RW was useful when blank CDs cost a fiver, but now that they only cost a few pence it's not such a big deal if you waste a few.

Your cup runneth under

The most feared error in CD burning is 'buffer underrun'. The writing process takes place in real time and the CD-R's buffer must always contain data to feed the laser. If the buffer empties, the CD becomes a coaster for your coffee table. The likelihood of a buffer underrun error increases as writing speeds increase. Large buffers, therefore, are A Good Thing.

In 1999 a new technology surfaced called Burn Proof, which supposedly stands for Buffer Under RuN error Proof, although it's a neat name anyway and has been trademarked by Sanyo. It's a function of the hardware and firmware in the CD-R/-RW drive and essentially puts the burning process into pause if the buffer empties during a burn without damaging the CD. Truly an excellent

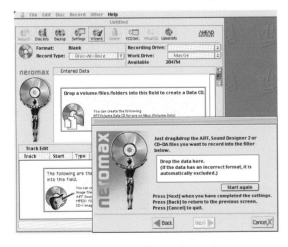

Ahead's NeroMax for the Apple Mac offers easy drag and drop audio CD creation.

Creating audio CDs doesn't get much easier than using Adaptec's Easy CD Creator. Drag files from the Explorer window to the Playlist. There's even a cute Helper to assist if you get stuck.

idea. You do need a Burn Proof drive to use this. Most modern drives tend to include the technology, and most software supports Burn Proof, too.

Give me more

Overburning sounds like it might be related to buffer underruns, but it's not. It's the process of squeezing a quart into a pint pot or, more specifically, the art of squeezing more than 74 minutes of audio onto a 74-minute CD. At least it was originally. Now you can buy oversized CD blanks such as R90 and R99 that promise playback times of up to 100 minutes. The extra data is achieved by putting the tracks closer together.

The overburning process requires that the CD-R be physically able to overburn and the CD-R software must support it, too. It's also generally considered a good idea to limit the writing speed to 2x or 4x.

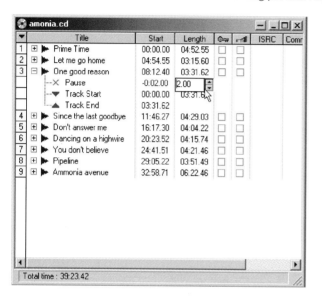

The main problem with oversized CDs, assuming you can burn them in the first place, is that they may not be recognised by all your playback systems. In fact, with any home-burned CD you run the risk of it not playing in a car multi-CD changer, for example, and this risk increases the more a CD is overburned. However, there are so many variables involved that you really need to try it out to see what the resulting CDs will play on.

Most people used overburning in order to duplicate commercial CDs that were longer than normal. If you keep your demands modest, such as overburning an R74 to 76 minutes, there's a greater likelihood they will play on other systems.

WaveLab makes it easy to adjust track start and end times, change the pause time, set Lock and Emphasis flags, and enter ISRC codes.

Code breaker

If you've delved into some of the more detailed CD-R software, you'll have noticed a range of codes and parameters that you can set and change.

- *ISRC* The International Standard Recording Code enables information about the country of origin, year of issue and serial number to be burned to the CD. It is generally only used on commercial recordings.
- *UPC* The Universal Product Code is a 13-digit catalogue number. Again, it's mainly used on commercial recordings.
- *Subcodes* This is where it gets interesting. There are eight subcode channels on each CD, labelled P to W. Channels R to W are used for CD graphics, while P and Q store information such as track start and sub-index information.

Mind your Ps and Qs

As PQ subcodes determine track times, you can change the times by changing the codes. The P channel indicates the start and end times of each track, while the Q channel provides timecode addresses. It also stores the state of the Protect or Lock flag, which prevents the CD being digitally copied, and the Emphasis flag. Emphasis is a basic noise-reduction process, but it's rarely used.

There is a host of rules about PQ codes, such as having silent frames before each track, and that sub-indexes should be early, but most software that lets you adjust these settings does so in a friendly manner. Multi-purpose CD-R software doesn't usually let you get this far down and dirty, which is why specialist audio software such as Sonic Foundry's CD Architect and Steinberg's WaveLab is a must for creating customised audio CDs.

A typical reason for messing with these settings is to change the gap between the tracks. The Red Book standard is two seconds, but you can make it longer or shorter. You can also record a 'live' session or join audio tracks together so they play continuously, but with track start positions inserted in the data so you can skip to any of the songs. This is where dedicated software comes to the fore. With CD Architect, for example, you can even crossfade between tracks – very professional!

Index linked

CDs can hold a maximum of 99 tracks. However, each track can be further marked with up to 99 index points. Again, with suitable software, you can drop an index into a track at any position.

Indices were first widely used by sample CD creators who would stuff 1,000 samples onto one CD in 99 tracks, each track typically having ten index points to make it easy to find individual samples. Another oft-touted use is in classical music to point out different sections in a piece.

Not all CD players recognise index points, however, and sometimes the hassle of using indices is more than it's worth. For whatever reason, indices are not in common use, but it's nice to know they're there.

You can quickly create audio CDs with 'ready-to-burn' software, but a little knowledge of the audio CD format and how audio tracks are assembled on a CD will enable you to create highly-customised CDs.

Tech terms

Run-in/Run-out blocks
Small pieces of data written at the start and end of each track when using TAO mode writing.

Frame
The smallest unit of data a CD drive can access, comprising 24 bytes of data, with sub-code and error correction.

CD-R
CD-Recordable. Can only be written to once.

CD-RW
CD-ReWritable, able to be written to and erased many times.

Further info

There's more information about audio CDs and CD formats on the web than you want to know. Work through these until mental fatigue sets in: www.disctronics.co.uk/technology/cdbasics/cd_intro.htm An excellent source of CD information containing copious amounts of information about CD formats and audio CD mastering.

www.burn-proof.com
contains everything you want to know about this technology.
www6.tomshadware.com/storage/20020411/index.html
has lots of information on overburning.
www.cdplant.se/eng/cdformatseng.htm

5

Cabling

Whether you're starting out with a home studio for your own recordings or growing your project studio, the main focus is naturally on what gear you're going to be using. And while we devote a great deal of time to which new sampler, keyboard or mixer to buy, often much less thought goes into how to connect them all together.

Cabling may not be very exciting, but it's a very important consideration, and one that needs to be seriously addressed from the outset. After all, if you've just parted with the best part of £1,500 of your hard-earned for a decent mixer and the latest in sampling technology, shouldn't you give a bit of thought to how you're going to get all those fantastic sounds out of the box and into your mix?

There are two main aspects to correctly cabling up your studio; the first of these is ensuring you get the best possible signal quality; the second is a practicality issue – how to keep it all neat and tidy and also have a flexible setup that doesn't need major replugging every time you use a different piece of kit.

Maintaining signal quality is an important issue. At every stage along its path, the signal is liable to degradation – long cable runs, cheap connectors and use of adaptors will all reduce the strength and quality of the signal, as will interference picked up along the way. Here are four ways to reduce signal degradation:

- Use balanced cables where possible. Balanced cables cancel out any hum and noise that may be picked up by the cables.
- Use the right cable for the job – don't use adaptors. Every 'junction' that the signal passes through is an opportunity for it to degrade.
- Keep cable runs as short as possible. Not only will this reduce noise, but the natural capacitance of audio cable causes a high-frequency rolloff effect over longer lengths. It also looks much neater…
- Use decent quality cables and plugs. Obvious really, but be aware: the salesman at your favourite music outlet may be offering you some cables for free to close a deal on the keyboard you've been eyeing, but chances are they'll be the cheapest of the cheap and often the best place to plug them in is directly into your dustbin.

Don't interfere

If your studio is computer based, then the chances are that you already own one of the most virulent interference-generating units available – the CRT monitor. They emit heaps of RF (Radio Frequency) interference, which can manifest itself as buzzing in your signal. To minimise this, make sure that your cables are the shielded variety, keep audio cable runs separate from mains cables and transformers, and if at all possible keep monitor screens on one side of the studio and cabling on the other.

Balancing act

There are two types of audio connections (and by that we're referring only to analogue connections): balanced and unbalanced. Unbalanced connections are often labelled as -10dB and the cables comprise a single core that carries the signal, surrounded by a ground connection. If the core picks up interference, it will manifest itself as noise.

Balanced connections (+4dB) have two cores, a positive and a negative, as well as a surrounding ground. Both the positive and the negative carry the signal, but within the cable they are exactly out of phase with each other (ie. 180 degrees out of phase). At the receiving end, the phase of the negative terminal is inverted and added to the positive. Both cores will pick up any interference, and when the phase reversal is performed, the noise will be cancelled out. The summation of the two signals also means that balanced connections offer a much stronger signal. See the diagram at the top of the page opposite for a graphical explanation of the process.

Unbalanced connections usually take the form of phono plugs or standard mono jack plugs. Balanced connections are usually in the form of XLR connectors or stereo (TRS) jacks.

Where possible, opt for oxygen-free cable as this prevents the gradual degradation of the cable caused by oxidation of its copper core. Most cable is also screened to minimise interference. Screening is usually a layer of PVC tubing inside the cable itself, within which the core(s) and ground are located, but foil screening is also available. Foil screening offers better rejection of interference, but is not as flexible, so it's best suited to installations where it's not going to be moved around too much. If you're wiring speakers to an amp, go for heavy-duty speaker cable as there's a lot of current flowing through it.

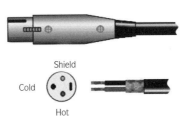

Balanced XLR connector wiring.

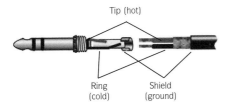

Balanced stereo jack wiring.

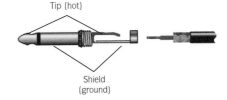

Unbalanced mono jack wiring.

Reducing noise with balanced cabling. Figure 1: noise is picked up by both the positive and negative cores.

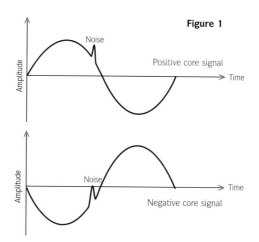

Figure 1

Figure 2: one signal is phase-reversed at the connection – the audio signals are in phase, but the noise is now out of phase.

Figure 3: summing the two signals produces an increase in signal amplitude and the noise is cancelled.

Figure 2

Figure 3

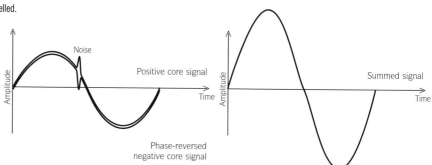

The choice of plug is equally important – steer clear of plastic moulded plugs, and go for the gold-plated versions if you can afford them. Neutrik connectors are a luxury, but they're well worth the investment. They're a one-piece construction – unlike cheaper plugs, which are assembled – that makes them much more durable if they're being plugged and unplugged a lot.

Make the connection

In terms of the actual connections found on the equipment, there are three types that are in common use. The 1/4-inch jack is probably the most common connection found in the studio, and will be familiar to anyone who has ever plugged in an instrument because it's the standard plug on the end of a guitar lead. 1/4-inch jacks can be either balanced or unbalanced and are either stereo (TRS) or mono jacks.

The presence of a jack socket is generally a good indicator that you're dealing with a line-level signal, and it's the most common connector you'll find on a mixer's line inputs, auxiliary sends and returns, tape returns, monitor outputs and buss outputs. Inputs and outputs from effects units and dynamics processors, outputs from preamps, outputs from keyboards and modules will, for the most part, also be on 1/4-inch jacks.

The second most common connector in the studio is the XLR. Most mic-level inputs will be handled by XLR connectors, but the format is also used for line-level connections on high-end equipment. The advantages of using line-level XLR connectors in the pro arena are that the recognisable male and female connectors indicate signal flow direction (signal flows from the male connector – the one with the pins – to the female connector), and the plugs physically lock into the sockets. The separate pins also give a good surface area for contact and reduce interference.

Probably the least common connection in the studio is the phono or RCA plug. Because it can't carry a balanced connection, RCA connectors tend to appear on lower-end equipment; it's essentially a consumer hi-fi standard. However, for space reasons, many computer soundcards use phono connectors, especially PCI cards where the inputs and outputs are directly mounted on the back of the card rather than on an external breakout box. DAT machines, CD players and recorders and even the two-track inputs on mixers are also commonly phono connectors.

Practical magic

Having to ferret around in the back of a rack, or constantly juggle connections every time you need to use a different piece of gear is a fantastic way of taking the momentum out of any session. This is where a patchbay can come in handy. In a commercial studio, where flexibility is paramount, it's common for every conceivable input and output to appear in a patchbay, but this may not be strictly necessary in a home or project studio.

Remember that by using a patchbay you're introducing more connections to your signal chain, as well as increasing the distance between source and destination. It's a false economy to opt for the cheapest patchbays because they often use poor-quality connectors. Use the patchbay where it will be useful, and plug in direct if you think the cable won't be plugged and unplugged very frequently. Remember that a balanced patchbay is also capable of handling phantom power, so you can use it for preamps too.

To keep things as neat as possible, try to use looms wherever you can. Not only is this a much neater solution than individual cables, but it can often work out slightly cheaper, too. If you record quite a bit of acoustic material, consider buying a small stage box and multicore cable as this will alleviate a lot of plugging and unplugging of mics, and trails of cables across your studio floor. Most music shops will carry some stock looms or multicores, but there are companies, such as Leisure Lynx and VDC, that will custom-build whatever lengths and plugs you need. Or if you're a bit handy with a soldering iron, it's perfectly possible to build all the cabling yourself; you can buy all the connectors, cabling and even webbing to make looms from cabling suppliers.

The best way to avoid

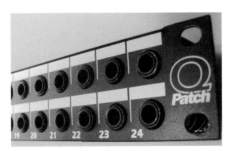

A patchbay will improve the flexibility of your connectivity, but it may not be strictly necessary.

Tech terms

Loom

A collection of cables, usually between 8 and 24, bound together in one outer 'jacket'. Much less messy than individual cables and useful when cabling units that have multiple outputs.

Stage box

A series of XLR or jack sockets mounted on a box, attached to a length of multicore cable and terminated with plugs, either at a desk or patchbay.

Interference

Unwanted noise that's picked up by the conductive cores of audio cable. Usually manifested as audible buzzing or hummming. Common causes are computer screens and power adaptors.

Ground

A common connection against which signal amplitudes can be measured. The equivalent of earth in electrical circuits.

cabling headaches and an expensive recabling job further down the line is to plan ahead – use looms from the outset, invest in a patchbay as soon you foresee your needs growing, and buy quality cabling whenever you buy something new.

Further info

More about balanced cables
www.whirlwindusa.com/tech01.html
www.audiomidi.com/classroom/general/cables.cfm

General information
Project Studios: A More Professional Approach by Philip Newell
Basic Home Studio Design by Paul White (Editor)

Product websites
www.leisure-lynx.com
www.vdctrading.com

Compression types

If a single piece of studio gear had to be distinguished as the ultimate tool, the compressor would be it. Put simply, compression can turn an average mix – with instruments fighting against one another – into one that gels and performs well on almost any system it's played on.

Given the variety of tasks compression is used for, it's no surprise that compressors come in many different designs, from the classic FET and opto compressors so popular in the 60s and 70s, through to today's digital and VCA compressors. As you'd expect, though, no one size fits all, and combining and contrasting these designs is key to a better-sounding mix.

Back to basics

Despite the many different approaches to compression, the processes that lie behind them are identical. Compression, in its purest sense, is a form of automated gain control: a device responds to the level of sound at its input and attenuates the output accordingly. The two main parameters involved are threshold (the point at which the compression, applied in the form of gain reduction, begins) and ratio (which defines the strength of gain reduction taking place above the threshold). In assessing and applying the required amount of gain reduction, the compressor needs a specific piece of circuitry known as the gain cell, or gain-control element. It is this element that forms the principal difference between the various types of compressor (opto, FET and VCA, for example) available today.

Moving beyond threshold and ratio, the other two variables are attack and release, which determine how fast the compressor responds. With fast

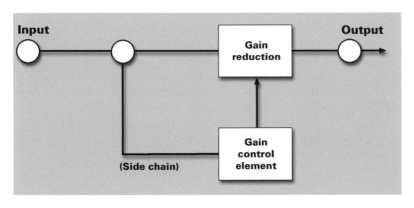

The heart of a compressor is the gain-control element. How the control element works and what effect this has on the compression and quality of sound differs with different compressor designs.

Software re-creations of original vintage compressors have come a long way. UAD-1's Fairchild 670 is faithfully modelled on the original 1950s Variable Mu

attack and release times, the compressor moves in and out of compression quickly, squashing transients and creating a pumping effect. With a slower setting, the compression is smoother, but some instantaneous, high-amplitude elements (such as transients) may slip through the net.

Interestingly, as well as having specific controls for attack and release times, the various designs also exhibit different qualities of responsiveness, so one type of compressor may be favoured for its fast attack, while another is enamoured for is gentle, discrete operation. Therefore, choosing the right type of compression involves picking both the right type of compressor as well as establishing the correct settings.

Optical illusions

Early compressor designs struggled with the limitations of rudimentary electronics, often using ingenious solutions to solve what are, by today's standards, relatively simple problems. Of course, many of these designs were riddled with imperfections and an overall lack of flexibility – but in retrospect, this also accounts for the continued appeal of vintage compressors. Optical compressors (also known as opto compressors), use a small light cell in the form of an LED (early devices crudely employed filament light bulbs) to translate sound energy into light energy. The strength of the light is determined by a photocell, which drives the gain reduction.

The unique qualities of opto compressors – like the classic Teletronix LA-2A Levelling Amplifier – are defined by how the LED and photocell respond to the incoming signal. The system has an innate lag in it, so although the audio signal may quickly fall in level, the light element will take some time to return to its lowest state, resulting in a slow release.

Another interesting factor governing the release times is that if the light element is active for a long time (in other words, if it's in a constant state of compression) the photocell will take longer to dim. Equally, at the other end of the equation, the time the light takes to react to fast transients is somewhat sluggish, often resulting in some peaks slipping through.

So, with all these inherent problems, why do people spend upwards of £2,000 on compressors like the Teletronix? Certainly, at the time they were first built, the opto circuit produced little added harmonic distortion, but their real charm was how musical an opto's compression sounded. In addition to this, their use as levelling amplifiers implies a low threshold and medium ratio, so that the compressor spends most of its time 'in compression' – massaging the whole of the programme material (rather than just the loud bits) into a more consistent overall dynamic.

Optical compression has had a bit of a revival in recent years, with models produced by Joe Meek and Focusrite. The Teletronix LA-2A, however, is

Bill, FETs and VCAs

To create faster, more responsive compressors, designers such as Bill Putnam moved on to explore the use of FETs (field-effect transistors) as the gain-control element. The main advantage with FETs is their incredible speed at reacting to fast transients (the very aspect optos were so bad at), making them much more suitable for heavier compression and limiting applications. Undoubtedly, the best example of a FET compressor – and possibly one of the finest compressors ever built – is the Urei 1176, technically know as a limiting (rather than levelling) amplifier because of its effectiveness in limiting applications.

FETs, however, weren't without their flaws, being both expensive to build and prone to some harmonic distortion and amplitude-modulation artefacts at extreme settings. However, this didn't stop the 1176 becoming a studio mainstay.

The eventual solution lay in the use of the ubiquitous VCA (voltage-controlled amplifier) as the gain-control element. VCA technology offered the best performance of the three types, with delicate control over all aspects of the compression. VCAs were also much cheaper to manufacture, and the idea of installing individual compressors on each channel of a console became financially viable.

Mu Mu Land

Beside the three main types discussed, there are other sub-branches of compressor types. The Manley Labs Stereo Variable Mu limiter/compressor is an interesting example of a tube-based solution. The Variable Mu design doesn't directly support a physical ratio control; instead, the harder the device is pushed, the greater the ratio of compression. Because of the valve circuitry and the gentle way the Variable Mu engages in gain reduction, these types of compressor are often the preferred choice for stereo-buss compression.

In a branch of its own is Empirical Lab's Distressor – a modern compressor that deliberately seeks to impart the non-linearity of many vintage compres-

The Manley Labs Stereo Variable Mu limiter/compressor doesn't have a conventional ratio control. Instead, the ratio changes in direct response to the signal level entering the unit, as shown in the gain reduction graph.

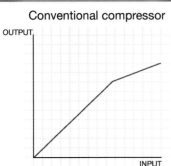

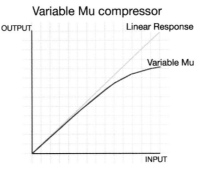

The classic FET compressor – the Urei 1176, as designed by Bill Putnam. At the time, the FET design produced a far quicker response than that of existing optical compressors.

Tech terms

Soft-knee compression

The 'knee' of a compressor defines its transition (in respect to the ratio) from no compression to compression. In a soft-knee compressor, the ratio will begin to slowly increase as it moves up to the threshold (say, 1.5:1), only reaching its full ratio (perhaps 3:1) just after the threshold level.

Look-ahead compression

Digital compressors feature the ability to look ahead and spot any problem transients before they have to compress them. To do this, a look-ahead compressor will use a temporary storage buffer, which can introduce a small amount of latency.

Brick-wall limiter

A brick-wall limiter uses a small attack time to grab any signals exceeding its given threshold. In short, these limiters will not let any signal exceed a particular level.

sors. To achieve this, the Distressor uses a combination of both a compressor and distortion unit. The Distressor has many fans, including big-name mixers such as Bob Clearmountain and the Lord-Alge brothers.

A digital future

Time moves on, though, and many engineers and musicians today will be working in the digital domain. Digital compression has certainly made some big jumps in the last ten years, providing us with both some of the most accurate compression tools as well as the ability to replicate – relatively faithfully – the vintage compressors we've discussed here. Universal Audio's UAD-1, for example, includes versions of the 1176, LA-2A and Fairchild 670 – two of which (the LA-2A and 1176) are still manufactured as hardware devices.

Compression is, undoubtedly, an engineer's best friend. But, like any good circle of friends, it's worth mixing with different types of people to bring variety and interest to your life. Thankfully, the choice today – whether it's opto, VCA or FET, powered by either software or hardware – couldn't be more varied, giving us the potential to create some truly stunning mixes.

Further info

To hear compression in its full glory, take a listen to: Led Zeppelin IV, Blood Sugar Sex Magik (Red Hot Chilli Peppers), Mezzanine (Massive Attack).
An interesting interview with Andy Johns about vintage compressors:
www.uaudio.com/webzine/2003/april/index8.html
As a counterbalance to the abuse of compression, read Bob Katz's articles on the Digital Domain site:
www.digido.com
To find out more about some of the products mentioned here:
www.uaudio.com
www.empiricallabs.com
www.manleylabs.com

Compressing audio

Digital audio exists in different forms and at different levels of quality. A regular audio CD contains data sampled at 44.1kHz/16-bit resolution. DVD-A discs sample at up to 192kHz/24-bit resolution. In this example, the DVD-A contains more information. If you digitised the same track from each disc onto a computer, the version from the DVD would be a larger file. More information means bigger files, and less information means, of course, a smaller file size. An audio file sampled at a higher resolution and bit rate will generally sound better, and have greater clarity than an audio file sampled at a lower resolution or bit rate. Given that 60 seconds of CD-quality stereo audio creates a 10MB file, digitising an entire audio CD 60 minutes long would use around 600MB of space.

The first effective audio compression technique was developed in the late 1980s by the Fraunhofer Institute in Germany, but it didn't take off until the late 1990s due to the lack of a decent player. The now-ubiquitous MP3 stands for MPEG Audio Layer 3. MPEG itself is the Motion Picture Experts Group, which was responsible for standardising other video formats such as MPEG1 (VCD and web) and MPEG2 (DVD Video). MP3 works by analysing and shrinking audio files with only a small perceptible loss in sound quality, although this is dependent on compression rate. The explosion in the popularity of MP3, and the resulting rise of file-sharing networks such as Napster and Kazaa is well documented. It has gone hand-in-hand with the age of mass personal computing, and even been the basis of marketing campaigns such as Apple's Rip, Mix, Burn for the iMac.

Stream or download?

Making backups of your own CDs to MP3 to store on your computer or iPod is only a small part of what's possible for audio compression. Audio for the web is now very popular. There are two main types of web audio – download and streaming. A download file must be fully downloaded or played in a web browser, and is the preferred format for individuals and companies who want people to be able to download, keep and maybe distribute samples, tunes or spoken-word material.

A streaming file is either embedded in a browser window or downloads a tiny 'link' file that opens an application such as RealPlayer or Windows Media Player.

Cleaner enables you to specify QT, Windows Media and RealPlayer streaming servers for streaming files.

27

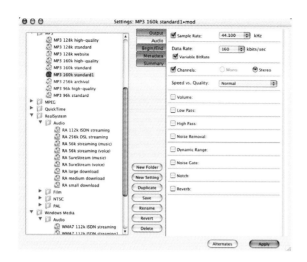

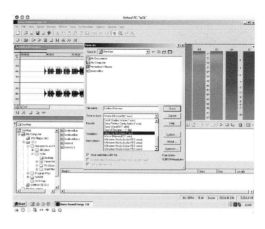

Wave editors such as Sound Forge can read and export a huge range of audio formats and codecs.

Cleaner supports video and audio coding in many different formats, with precise controls.

Streaming audio is not stored on your computer – every time you play it, it's streamed afresh from a server, so you never have a copy of it. To compensate for network instability, streaming audio uses 'buffering' to store a proportion of the data in a cache so that it's always downloading a few seconds ahead of what it's playing.

Streaming formats are favoured by record companies because the user doesn't get to keep a copy of the music. There are other advantages, such as the ability of most streaming players to auto-detect your connection speed and stream at a suitable bandwidth. In fact, most major web audio formats can be set up to work with either type of format. MP3, QuickTime Audio, RealAudio and Windows Media Audio files can all be encoded to stream or download.

It's also worth noting that to properly stream a file you need access to a streaming server. Some encoding software enables you to include data in your files such as copyright, web links and copy protection, as well as the ability to perform fades, gain adjustments or effects as files are encoded.

Get compressed

Compressing audio is a relatively straightforward process. Cleaner by Discreet Software is a powerful encoding package for PC or Mac, which supports customisable, multi-format coding. Specifically for the PC, there is the free and powerful Windows Media Encoder, which handles audio or video coding. Mac users may export from QuickTime Player or iTunes, or use QuickTime Broadcaster in OSX Server.

The most common form of audio compression, used by many of us for archiving our own music collections, creating playlists and libraries, and publishing our own music online is, of course, MP3. The standard bit rate for encoding MP3s is 128kbps at 44.1kHz, although this can produce artefacting in the top end – usually cymbals appear to be 'phasing' if the compression is too heavy. MP3 compresses at around 10:1, so a four-minute song at 128kbps would typically occupy 3.5MB space. Most find that a bit rate of 160-192kbps produces a file that sounds much closer to the original, with only a small increase in file size.

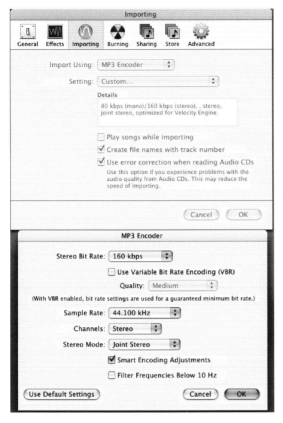

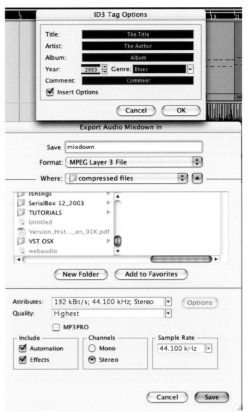

Apple's free iTunes can encode to AIFF, .WAV, MP3 or AAC and use Variable Bit Rate for smaller file sizes.

Some sequencers, such as Cubase SX, can export compressed files directly and embed ID tags.

The great strength of MP3 is that everyone uses it and can read it. It has been absorbed into many multimedia applications. When exporting a Shockwave movie from Macromedia Director or Flash, any audio is converted to MP3 at a chosen bit rate for effective web streaming.

Within MP3 itself, there are further algorithms to streamline file sizes. Variable Bit Rate (VBR) encoding, if selected, analyses a file and bases its compression on the amount of signal present at any given point. Hence a music track would only benefit marginally from VBR because it plays constantly. But a spoken-word track encoded at, say, 96kbps with VBR would result in a much smaller file at a similar quality. When a person takes one of their frequent breaks while speaking, there is virtually no signal present, so the MP3 doesn't need to record much data. Multiply this by the hundreds of short pauses in a radio news broadcast, for example, and you can throw away quite a lot of unnecessary silence. But VBR should be used with care as it's incompatible with some players, and the final file size can vary with the complexity of the original file.

Tech terms

Ripping

Copying audio files from an audio CD to a hard drive for conversion to MP3 or any other compressed format.

Lossy compression

Reducing audio file sizes by throwing away data that is inaudible to the human ear. Also used by the MiniDisc format

Buffering

When streaming audio over networks, data is stored and played from a buffer in the host application, constantly updated, to prevent stalling. Used by all major streaming applications.

Codec

An algorithm that provides a framework for interpreting data, usually audio or video. For example, you need the MPEG4 codec installed to play content encoded using MPEG4.

The competition

MP3 is the biggest, but by no means the only, format available. Here's are some of the other formats and how they work:

Windows Media

Similar to MP3, but proprietary to Windows and playable only by Windows Media Player. It uses Windows Media codecs, and version 9 includes some Digital Rights Management features. Good encoding tools are available, and although usable on the Mac, they're only really effective under Windows. Produces good-quality results with relatively small file sizes. Equally useful for download and streaming.

Ogg Vorbis

Open-source alternative to MP3, and it's free (not licensed). Players and encoders are available for download and the format initially promised great results, but has somewhat disappeared from view, possibly due to a lack of backing from a big name. Still supported as an export option in many sequencers and wave editors.

RealAudio

A streaming architecture developed by RealNetworks. As with RealVideo, you need the RealPlayer program to view this format. Only higher-end programs, such as Cleaner, Sound Forge or RealProducer, will encode to the Real format, so you're unlikely to find many freeware encoders. Real content is well suited to streaming and embedding in browsers, and supports SMIL (Synchronized Multimedia Integration Language), which enables Real content to control other elements in a webpage such as URL page flips, loading multiple movies and so on while streaming. Not really used in multimedia because it's optimised for web streaming, and better suited to the pro web producer than the hobbyist. RealAudio tends to be used by record labels, online news stations and online radio stations for content distribution. Real content can't be edited or recompressed.

AAC

Advanced Audio Coding was introduced in 2001 as a higher-quality alternative to MP3. Featuring built-in copy protection, it offers better quality at smaller sizes. It's still being adopted, but has been embraced by Apple as the format of choice for distributing music throughout the iTunes music store, and can be encoded directly from iTunes. Increasingly, MP3 players are AAC-compliant.

MPEG4

A relative of the DivX video codec, MPEG4 is used in 3G video phones and supported on computers by QuickTime 6.3 or higher, and WMP 8 or higher. Provides very small files, but can be lower quality, and not readable by everyone.

Alternative codecs

Within the bracket of AIFF, WAV, MP3 and QuickTime audio files there are options to use other codecs as compressors while keeping the file extension the same. These depend on which codecs are installed on your system, but include MACE, Quaalcomm, IMA, u-law and a host of others that are too specialised to warrant coverage here. As a rule, you should only use them if you know specifically why you're using them. In your encoder, look under the list of codec options to see what you have available.

Of course, within each of these formats there are options to precisely customise your encoded files. Bit rate, sample rate, stereo/mono, VBR, codec, software version, metadata, ID tags and data rate can all be specified for precise control over how your files turn out. For most, presets will do the trick, but for more advanced users there are now unprecedented levels of control.

A word of wisdom, though – keep it generic. If the world uses MP3, you should use it, too. After all, you want everyone to be able to play your material. Web surfers won't persist for very long if they get a file that won't open – they'll just delete it. By compressing correctly and using platform-friendly formats, you can reach a much wider audience for your music via the web. But don't publish in just one format – use WMA, Real (if you can) and QuickTime so everyone can hear you.

Further info

Cleaner software and background on compression at
www.discreet.com
plus Windows Media encoder free at
www.microsoft.com
Shareware converters aplenty at
www.hitsquad.com/smm
Detailed technical MP3 information is at
www.mp3-tech.org
Links to many sources on sound processing and compression
www.mathtools.net/Applications/DSP/Sound_and_Speech_Processing

Compression

Compression is both the least glamorous and the most important effect on the rack. The part it plays is subtle and essential, bringing out lost nuances in lead lines, making vocals more intimate and adding vigour to rhythm tracks. Not bad for something that's essentially an automatic volume control.

Compressors alter the dynamics of an audio signal, making the quiet sounds louder and the loud sounds quieter, thereby smoothing out the total volume range. This has a number of recognisable effects. Sustain is increased in acoustic instruments as the volume of the decaying note is amplified. Louder peaks are 'rounded off' in some versions of the effect, creating a feeling of warmth in a track. Other compressors clip signals at the louder end, adding crunch to rhythm or guitar tracks. When pushed to the limit, compression can add rhythmic pulses to a track or even change the tonal qualities of an instrument.

The most obvious of this understated collection of effects is the illusion of increased loudness. Compressing a vocal or instrument evens out those troughs in volume that make our brains strain to piece together a sound.

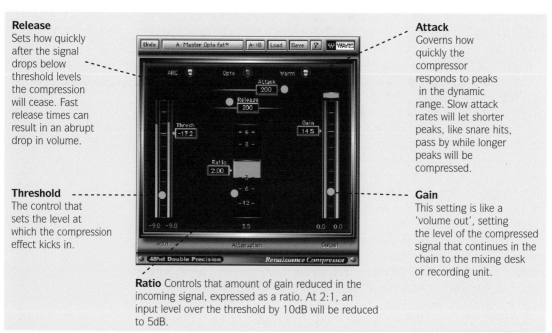

Release
Sets how quickly after the signal drops below threshold levels the compression will cease. Fast release times can result in an abrupt drop in volume.

Threshold
The control that sets the level at which the compression effect kicks in.

Attack
Governs how quickly the compressor responds to peaks in the dynamic range. Slow attack rates will let shorter peaks, like snare hits, pass by while longer peaks will be compressed.

Gain
This setting is like a 'volume out', setting the level of the compressed signal that continues in the chain to the mixing desk or recording unit.

Ratio Controls that amount of gain reduced in the incoming signal, expressed as a ratio. At 2:1, an input level over the threshold by 10dB will be reduced to 5dB.

With everything at roughly the same volume, we find it easier to pick out every note or beat, even when other instruments surround that sound.

Machine language

All professional studios will use either analogue or digital hardware compression, often both. The technology behind the analogue variety isn't too different from guitar or keyboard amplifiers and they fall into the same two categories as a result: valve-powered or solid-state units. But hybrid types that combine both technologies are also available, simultaneously taking advantage of the greater control afforded by circuit board-based units and the audio warmth of valve equipment. But whichever type of equipment is being used, compression is always achieved through gain adjustment – altering the signal to bring it within a specified limit. In many analogue systems the process will use Voltage Controlled Amplification (VCA), a method where a consistent, adjustable voltage is used to control the variable voltage of the incoming audio signal.

Digital compressors are more akin to samplers, converting the sound input to a digital signal, then measuring and adjusting the dynamic range mathematically. Some units can be used to pinpoint and isolate sets of individual frequency ranges in a process called 'multi-band' compression. This enables you to add different levels of compression to different parts of the signal, so you can, for example, add heavy, narrow compression at the bass end with more dynamic range at the top. This makes it a great tool in post production.

If you're working on a computer or in a digital studio, you'll probably be using software compressors. These work in a similar way to the digital hardware devices we've just discussed (which are essentially single-purpose computers). Although many musicians swear by analogue hardware, digital hardware and software compression have reached an advanced level. Using similar technology to that used by software synthesizers and some plug-ins, digital units can now emulate a range of the most famous analogue compressors of old. This is especially handy when you consider that buying one of the more sought-after analogue units, whether it be a modern or vintage modern model, would probably bankrupt all but the most affluent of musicians.

The PreSonus CL44, a rack-mounted studio compression unit includes a special 'optical' mode to emulate vintage compressors – although it's not cheap at around £500. Another option is Universal Audio's UAD1 DSP card, which includes Vintage Compressors, a software solution that models the respected Teletronics LA2A compressor, among others. Again though, at £880 it's hardly an impulse buy.

All these units offer different results. Older valve models give a 'warmer', more natural sound, while solid-state models traditionally are more accurate and aggressive across set frequency ranges. The digital models also have the benefit of being highly configurable and controllable.

Setting the controls

As well as the distinctive sound signatures of the different unit types, a standard set of controls gives you additional influence over the results. Like most effects, the 'input level' is the first control you'll encounter, but in compression it has a greater role than in some other processors. The next knob on the plate is usually a 'threshold' control, enabling you to set the level where compression kicks in. When used in tandem with the input level it enables you to select a dynamic range within the signal to be compressed.

While these controls set levels, the 'ratio' control is where you really take control of the process. This determines the amount of compression that's applied to that range. It's called a ratio control because it expresses the output of the process as a ratio of the input signal. So, a compression ratio of 2:1 halves the dynamic range over the threshold level. If a peak level over the threshold is at 12dB, for example, this will be compressed to 6dB. At a ratio of 3:1 the signal would be compressed to 4dB – a third of the original signal.

Everyday use

Compression can be applied to individual instruments at different stages of the recording process. If you're recording a bass instrument directly through the mixing desk or into a home studio setup, it can sometimes be a good idea to put a compressor between the instrument and the input. You can try quite high ratios to smooth out the peaks caused by the lowest notes, starting at 8:1 and experimenting with threshold and ratio to get the best results. Rhythm tracks and live drums benefit from the same treatment, especially when you're trying to record an entire kit with just a couple of mics. Professional studios frequently compress each part of the kit separately.

Before and after: In the above image we see an unprocessed sound wave – a guitar sample with peak notes and plectrum hits. Below we see the same wave after a dose of compression – those peaks have been smoothed out.

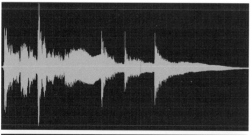
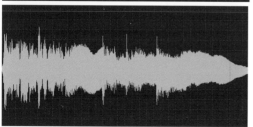

Vocal lines, capable of expressing the gamut of human emotions, absolutely cry out (and whisper) for compression. They're sometimes compressed as they're being recorded, again to prevent clipped peaks that may lead to distortion in the recording medium. Don't, however, be tempted to compress vocals too hard while recording; any additional compression you require can always be added later.

Really, just about any instrument can benefit from a little compression. Rhythm guitars and strummed acoustics respond well – although lead lines are often compressed already with distortion. Even sequenced music, predominantly using electronic instruments can be improved. Try aggressive compression on tracks where the rhythm and bass are louder in the mix to bring up the overall levels. Some even advocate compressing mixdowns before mastering. The argument

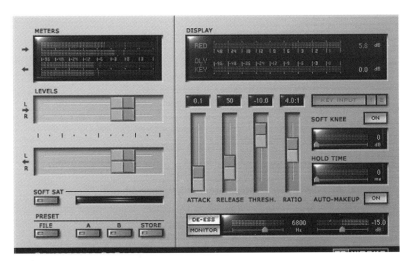

TC DeX32: A software-based compressor that behaves very much like its ardware cousins, down to the polished steel effect front panel.

goes that a final layer of compression enables you to cut the track at its maximum loudness. This is a matter of taste, but it probably works best on harder-hitting tunes.

Experimentation is the best the way to find out how compression will improve your work. Once you've got a good handle on it, your tunes will be more professional in finish, slicker in sound and with a clarity that's hard to achieve by any other means.

Tech terms

Soft and Hard Knee

Some compressors cut in noticeably at a specific point. We refer to this as Hard Knee compression. Soft Knee compression is a characteristic of valve systems, where the effect is applied progressively over a volume range, both before and after the threshold level. This lends a warmer, more 'rounded' sound. Modern units offer control over these characteristics.

Pumping

In addition to the controls we mention in the main article, compressors also have attack and release settings. When these are turned up high – causing compression to kick in and out more quickly – you can hear the volume rising and falling. Used on rhythmic tracks this effect is called pumping and can add extra oomph to your beats.

Side Chain

Some units enable you to attach a second 'input' or chain an additional effect through your compressor. This can be used to affect the compression levels processed. Similar in operation to an effects loop, you could side chain an equaliser to your compressor to narrow the affected frequency range. This is an old-school method for removing the sibilant 's' sound from vocals, or to smooth the peaks of hard consonants like 'p' and 'b'.

Copyright

With the rapid growth of the internet and the explosion of digital distribution – in all its forms, not just music – more and more people are becoming concerned about, and increasingly involved in, the issue of copyright protection. In fact, we hear so much about the subject these days that you could be forgiven for thinking that it's purely a 21st-century phenomenon. However, the first people to raise the issue of copyright were the scholars of Ancient Greece and the Roman Empire – and although they succeeded in achieving due recognition for their efforts, they didn't actually have any economic rights. In other words, anybody could copy and sell the scholar's work without asking his permission first. But, of course, without the technology to print the works anyway, the issue of piracy probably didn't arise.

The birth of piracy

With the invention of the printing press in the Middle Ages, everything changed. Until that time, the majority of manuscripts (both text and music) were of a religious nature and were usually hand-copied by monks. By the middle of the 17th century, though, a flourishing printing industry had been established. Cheap commercial printing inevitably led to piracy, and to protect the printers, King Charles II introduced the Licensing Act of 1662. But this Act was as much about regulating the content of books as it was about piracy, and books suspected of containing any anti-church or anti-government sentiments were most likely to be seized.

It wasn't until 1710 that copyright was properly enshrined in law as an Act of Parliament – for the first time anywhere in the world. Called the Statute of Anne, the new law contained two important new concepts: firstly, the author of the work became the automatic owner of the copyright; and secondly, the principle of a fixed term of protection for published works was introduced. These fundamental concepts remain in place

The MCPS website provides both a general overview of copyright issues plus in-depth information, available as a download.

today as part of the Copyright, Designs & Patents Act of 1988, which forms the framework for current UK copyright law.

The legalities

Lawyers refer to copyright as a property right that exists in original literary, musical, artistic and dramatic works (including computer software). It also exists in films, sound recordings and broadcasts.

It's worth noting that in the UK, if you write a song, the words and music are protected separately. As you'd expect, the score is classed as a musical work, but the lyrics are categorised as a literary one.

Obviously, anything you create must take a material form of some kind; you can't just copyright an idea. So, your ideas must be expressed – either written down, or recorded in some other way. For example, if you compose an original piece of music, the moment it's notated on paper or recorded to tape or CD, you – as the composer – automatically own the copyright to the work.

Contrary to popular belief, you're not required by law to register your creative endeavours. The copyright arises automatically the moment the work exists in a tangible form. That's all very well, of course, but what if somebody copies your song and has a massive hit with it? To initiate legal action against them, you'll have to prove that you composed the song in the first place. So, how do you prove ownership? There are a number of ways…

Date it

First and foremost you need to establish a specific date for the creation of your song. One way of doing this is to deposit a copy of your work with either a bank or a solicitor. In both cases there will be a charge for the service.

A much cheaper way is to send a copy of your song to yourself, by registered post. Of course, when the envelope arrives, you mustn't open it. Just keep it in a safe place. Also, if you write lots of songs and you adopt this method of registering them, it's a good idea to clearly label the envelopes with the titles. That way, in the event of a dispute, you'll know exactly which envelope to open when you arrive in court. That said, some lawyers will tell you that posting registered parcels to yourself is not the best method, arguing that it's easy to falsify and may be inadmissible in a court of law. However, the MCPS (Mechanical Copyright Protection Society) still recommends this as a valid method of dating your work.

As mentioned earlier, due to the internet and digital distribution in general, increasing numbers of businesses and individuals are seeking copyright protection for their documents and logos (you can't copyright a name by the

UK©CS
The UK Copyright Service

Register my copyright
Do I need to register?
How do I protect my work?
My account
Copyright Information
Our services
About us

The UK Copyright Service

The UK Copyright Service is a registration centre for original works by writers, musicians, artists, designers, software providers, authors, companies, organisations and individuals. Our service provides international protection by securing independent evidence that will help prove originality and ownership in any future claims or disputes.

Copyright information

Our information pages deal with copyright laws, infringement, notices, common questions and other issues.

Copyright fact sheets

P-01: UK copyright law
P-02: Protecting copyright
P-03: Using copyright notices
P-04: Copyright registration
P-05: Copyright infringement

Help pages

Common copyright questions
The answers to our most commonly asked questions about copyright.
Common registration questions
Answers to frequently asked questions about registration.

"The UK industry lost in excess of £9 billion to intellectual property theft in 2002, not including online copyright trademark infringements."

Source: FACT web site March 2004

Help to protect your work: Ensure it is properly marked, and that you have proper evidence to support legal action. More information...

The copyright registration centre

Registration is a powerful tool in combating infringement, and ensures you have the best evidence to protect your work and your rights.

Our registration centre provides the very best secured back up and archive management for your work, meaning we can ensure that you always have evidence to support you in any future disputes.

Whether you are a song writer, designer, artist, author, company or individual, if you produce original work, registration with UKCS is the fast, effective and low cost way to protect your work from copyright abuse.

How does copyright registration help?

Registering your songs with the UK Copyright Service is a low-cost method of protecting them from copyright infringement.

A convenient and legally binding way to copyright your compositions is to upload them as MP3-format files to the I Created It First website at www.icreate-ditfirst.com

way, but you can copyright a logo). Consequently, commercial organisations are springing up on the web to fulfil this demand – two of which are The UK Copyright Service and I Created It First. Both companies will register musical works, the former in CD, DVD and paper (scores) format, and the latter as mp3s (up to 3MB per work). Both companies charge a reasonable fee for the service. If you live in the US, all you have to do is register your songs with the US Copyright Office by filling out form SR and submitting it, along with two copies of your CD and $30.

Unlike the Ancient Greeks and the Romans, if you're a copyright holder these days, you do have economic rights. Also known as 'restricted rights', they enable you to copy your work and issue those copies to the public, either free or in the form of rentals. You can also perform, broadcast, show or play the work in public, as well as make adaptations to it. This may seem all rather obvious, but remember – if you are the copyright holder, nobody else can do or authorise any of these things without your prior permission.

Authors and owners

The Copyright Act states that the author of a work is the person who creates it. So, if you've composed a piece of music, you're considered the author and as such you are also the first owner of the copyright to the work. But copyright is considered to be property, and just as you can transfer ownership of your house to other parties, you can also transfer all or part of your copyright in a work to a publisher or an organisation such as the PRS (Performing Right Society). So, you see, the author is not always the copyright holder.

Instead of assigning your copyright to a song to another party, you also have the right to license it, either exclusively to another person or organisation, or to lots of different people. For example, you might have composed a piece of music which is suitable for use as a website theme tune. By granting a licence to lots of different website owners, you may generate more income from the tune than by allowing just one person to use it.

It might be that you write songs with a partner, in which case things become slightly more complicated. For example, if you both contributed towards the words and the music, your individual contributions are not distinct and you will both be considered, in the eyes of the law, to be joint copyright owners of the song. However, if you alone composed the music and your partner wrote all the lyrics without any collaboration, the differences are very clear and you will be considered to be separate copyright holders in each respect.

When you purchase a CD, there's more than one type of copyright ownership involved. These are: the actual physical owner of the product – usually the manufacturer of the CD (generally the record company); the owner of the musical or literary copyright embedded within it – usually the composer and publisher of the songs; and the copyright owner in the sound recording – usually the record producer. That's why, when you purchase a CD, you're not allowed to copy it or do anything else with it that's restricted to the copyright owners involved.

How long?

As mentioned earlier, the Act of Parliament known as the Statute of Anne introduced the principle of a fixed term of protection for published works. So how long does the copyright to your songs last? In the UK it lasts until 70 years after your death. And, if you also own the sound recording or perhaps a broadcast of the work, this will last until 50 years after you die.

Many people worry unnecessarily about the possibility of copyright infringement. After all, if someone copies your song and makes a great deal of money from it, if you've registered your work (and it really does belong to you), you'll be in a strong position to take legal action and recover the money you're owed – plus damages. That said, it's also a good idea to display a copyright statement with the work itself, which clearly demonstrates that you are the copyright owner.

More worrying, however, is the issue of piracy, where illegal copies of CDs and DVDs are reproduced en masse as counterfeits and sold on. MCPS has set up a special anti-piracy unit to deal with the problem. So, next time you're offered a dodgy CD, give them a call (anonymously, if you wish). Remember: if you make it big in the future, the pirates will probably be targeting you as well.

Tech terms

Automatic right
Copyright is automatic. As soon as a work is created in a material form it can be protected by copyright law.

License
The owner of copyright can give permission to another person to carry out an action (copy, perform and so on), without which it would otherwise infringe the copyright.

Moral right
The right to be acknowledged as the author of your work. Also the right to object to derogatory treatment of your work.

Further info

www.mcps-prs-alliance.co.uk/aboutcopyright
The MCPS/PRS website is your first stop for basic copyright information. If you need more details, download the comprehensive PDF document on the subject.

www.intellectual-property.gov.uk
The government-backed home of UK Intellectual Property On The Internet provides all the resources you need to find your way through the copyright jungle, including a list of useful publications.

www.wipo.int
The World Intellectual Property Organisation (WIPO) is an international organisation dedicated to promoting the use and protection of works of the human spirit. Based in Geneva, Switzerland, WIPO is a specialised agency of the United Nations.

www.hmso.gov.uk/acts/acts1988/Ukpga_19880048_en_1.htm
Copyright, Designs and Patents Act 1988. A UK government site that contains the complete legislation.

10 | Delay

In the world of music and music technology, timing is everything. Our perception of music and sound is inextricably linked to it: from the time taken for air molecules to vibrate (pitch), through to the duration between beats (tempo). In its simplest form, delay is nothing more than the manipulation of time: holding events electronically for a period of time before releasing them back into the signal path. Yet for something so seemingly straightforward, delay is a fundamental component of the majority of effects processors found in today's studios, including reverb, chorus and flange, alongside specific delay-based effects such as slapback, multi-tap, ping-pong and tape delay.

Delay comes in many shapes and forms – indeed, one theory behind the design and construction of Stonehenge is that it forms a primitive example of multi-tap delay, with the sound of Neolithic drums bouncing off the strategically placed stone pillars. More recently, rock'n'roll from the early 50s and dub music in the late 60s both used delay as a predominant feature – either for slapback vocals or to create the haunting, regenerative sound of tape delay. Even today, delay continues to push back the boundaries of music and sound design thanks to innovative software products such as Native Instruments' Spektral Delay.

On reflection

The continuing popularity of delay is directly linked to the way we perceive sound. Acoustically, we most commonly encounter delay as sounds reflected back from solid objects, such as buildings or the walls of a room. Due to the speed of the sound travelling to and from these objects, the early reflections are perceived as discrete repeats – or echoes – of the original sound, but at a lesser amplitude. In an enclosed space, the sound will continue to bounce around (from one wall to another), creating ever-more complex arrangements of reflections known as reverb – but that is another subject altogether. Outside, however, the reflections have less opportunity to bounce around, so you're more likely to perceive the echo as a few simple reflections.

We use these early reflections to define important qualities of spatial awareness: where the sound is in relation to us; what kind of space we are in (either inside or outside); and our proximity to walls and surfaces. Another important facet of the echo is its timbre, as different surfaces absorb differing amounts and frequencies of sound. Even with just a single echo, our brains can decode a complete awareness of space and the objects around us, something that we largely take for granted.

Sunny slapback

With or without a theoretical understanding of how the brain perceives sound, musicians, composers and engineers have all made use of delay. Take, for example, the simple act of combining two musicians: here, the delay created by players performing slightly out of sync with each other forms a thicker, more pleasing sound. This concept directly influenced the first use of delay in music production – that of slapback delay. Slapback (as employed by engineers such as Sam Phillips, working for Sun Records) exploited the timing differences between the record and playback heads of early tape machines, creating a distinctive 50–70millisecond delay often used on vocals and guitars.

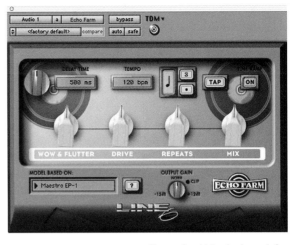

If you can't resist the classic sound of tape delay, there are plenty of competent software re-creations, including Line 6's Echo Farm, Logic Pro 7's Tape Delay and Steinberg's Karlette.

Slapback works by using the tape as a temporary storage medium, momentarily holding the sound before releasing it a few milliseconds later. The record head initially encodes the signal – as fluctuations in voltage – onto the tape. The playback head – separate from the record head and positioned a few inches further along the tape – picks up the voltage when the tape eventually reaches it and outputs the signal accordingly. Blending the sounds from the direct source and the tape machine produces the characteristic slapback effect, with further control available by altering the tape speed (moving from 15IPS to 7.5IPS would double the delay time). Best of all, the recorded signal sounds darker and slightly more distorted than the original sound, in a way that echoes the timbre of real-life early reflections.

Space echoes

As popular as the tape slapback effect became, its limitations prevented any thorough exploration of the possibilities of delay. Refining the technology, however, resulted in the now infamous Roland Space Echo, Maestro Echoplex and WEM Copycat tape delays, opening up further treatments and effects beyond that of slapback. Tape delay systems used the same principal technology as slapback, but added some significant enhancements, including the ability to fully vary the distance between the record and playback heads (and,

Slapback (left) is created by positioning the record and playback heads on a tape machine some distance apart. The distance between the heads and the

Flange (right) uses an LFO to modulate the delay time. Because the delay time is set initially very short (0–40ms) the result is a pronounced comb filtering combined with a sweeping movement.

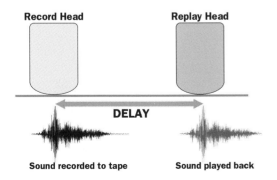

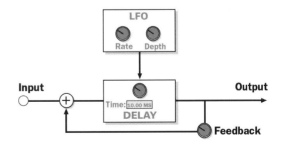

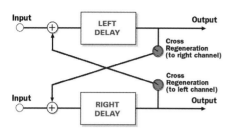

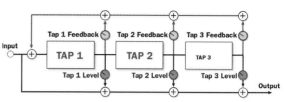

Multi-tap uses a series of delay lines to create complex arrangements of delay and feedback. Used carefully, multi-tap can (partly) approximate the sound of reverb.

Cross-feeding delay feedback/regeneration between the left and right channels creates ping-pong delay. The result is a delay that appears

therefore, create a variety of delay times) as well as the opportunity to add feedback, or regeneration.

Feedback sends a nominal amount of the signal back through the delay line to form a longer repetitive echo. Given the sonic distortions of tape and the high-frequency loss occurring on each repeat, extreme feedback settings became a popular feature, as exploited by dub artists such as King Tubby.

Call the fire brigade

With all the inherent performance limitations of tape delay (dirty heads, sticking tape and so on), a more dependable system of data storage needed to be developed. One such system, called a bucket-brigade delay, used a chain of capacitors to sample and hold an incoming voltage for a given duration of time – the longer the chain, the longer the delay. The imperfect nature of the capacitors, however, created the familiar problems of noise and distortion, so its inherent usefulness was limited. The solution was to use digital sampling, whereby the signal is digitally sampled, stored in RAM and then outputted accordingly.

Digital delay lines (DDL) finally offered full and precise control over the delay time (from milliseconds to seconds), with long delay times achievable thanks to increasingly powerful processors utilising large amounts of RAM. More complicated delay configurations could also be constructed in the digital domain, including ping-pong delay (where delays bounce from one side of the stereo image to another) and multi-tap delay (where a number of different delay lines with different delay times are combined). The only downside engineers became aware of was that digital delays – because they use exact replicas of the original sound – didn't sound quite as musical as tape delay. For that reason, a low-pass filter on the feedback path became essential to replicate the natural dampening that occurs both in the acoustic world and on tape.

Waves' SuperTap is a fine example of the contemporary digital delay. With six available taps, filtering, pan and feedback controls, SuperTap offers complete control over the effected signal.

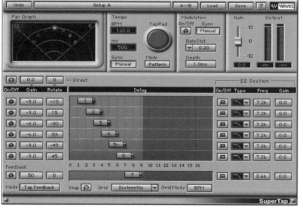

Too close for comfort

Where delays are particularly close to one another (less than 30ms, for example) the brain perceives the output as a single sound. What's more, the proximity of the two sounds creates a phase cancellation – the sound appearing thinner and weaker than the original version. Looked at through a spectral analyser, the phase characteristics appear as distinct notches – comb filtering – in the frequency spectrum, brought about through frequencies cancelling one another out. Used statically, the effect isn't that desirable or interesting, but by adding modulation (in the form of an LFO to modulate the delay time), the comb filtering moves to create the classic 'swoosh' of a flanger. As with conventional delay lines, feedback can be introduced, although in this case it intensifies the strength of the effect and the comb filtering taking place.

Moving the delay time of a modulated delay beyond 50ms creates the effect of chorus, although the pitch (of the delayed voice) also needs to be controlled by an LFO for a completely authentic re-creation. In essence, chorus takes us back to the concept of slapback – using short delay times to fool the listener into believing they're listening to more than one player. The important difference with chorus is that the modulation helps break up the effect by pseudo-randomising the delay time between two parts, so that the chorused part doesn't appear as a purely 'offset' version.

Resonators, RSS and beyond

Without modulation – and with plenty of feedback – short delays can also be made to resonate at a pitch defined by the delay time. Theoretically, a number of different delay lines could be stacked – each with its own delay time – to create a chord resonator. Many other popular sound processors also make discrete use of short delay to enhance stereo widths, create artificial 3D sound placements and so on. Roland's RSS system, for example, uses a combination of delays, filters and phase manipulation to place sounds behind the listener's head – without requiring extra speakers. BBE's Sonic Maximizer applies delay to frequencies below 150Hz to create a better alignment between treble and bass transients emitted from a loudspeaker.

Whereas other effects fall in and out of favour, delay has remained a vital process in modern music production. Clearly, its appeal is on many levels: its direct relation to the auditory world, the glorious lo-fi tones of the tape delay, and the accuracy and dexterity of the contemporary digital delay. If you could ever pick a 'desert island' effect, then delay would have to be it.

Further info

To find out more about the primitive acoustic qualities of Stonehenge, listen to:
www.bbc.co.uk/radio4/science/acousticshadows.shtml
For more information on tape delays:
www.loopers-delight.com/tools/oldechoplex/oldechoplex.html
www.uaudio.com/webzine/june/text/content4.html
www.vintagesynth.org/roland/re201.shtml
For more information on the pioneers of delay – Sam Phillips and King Tubby – visit:
www.history-of-rock.com/sam_phillips_sun_records.htm
www.jahsonic.com/KingTubby.html

Tech terms

Taps
Taps are a way of identifying multiple delay lines. In a multi-tap delay, for example, a unique tap number identifies each line and its associated time and feedback controls.

IPS
Inches per second. This denotes the speed of the tape on an analogue tape recorder. Generally, a faster speed ensures better recording quality; however, in the case of slapback, it varies the delay time.

Phase cancellation
Phase cancellation occurs when two (close) frequencies are summed together. If a 440Hz sine wave, for example, is combined with another 440Hz sine wave that's delayed by half a cycle, the result is silence.

Digital errors

In a time before digital recording, an engineer's job required actively spotting and preventing signal degradations that plagued analogue recording – albeit noise, distortion, wow, flutter or high-frequency generation loss. Now that we've all grown used to recording in the digital domain, our ears have, to some extent, switched off to many of these concerns – we simply trust that a digital recording will be a near flawless representation of the original sound. But beneath this thin veneer of digital perfection, things can easily go wrong. What's even more worrying, though, is that because digital recording does such a good job of papering over the cracks, you might not even be aware of degradation occurring – that is, until it's too late.

Ones and zeros

On the face of it, there should be little that can go wrong with digital recording. Indeed, the system was designed to address the 'fuzziness' of analogue recording – the zeros and ones of binary messages, for example, being far easier to discern than the continuous fluctuations of voltage used in analogue recording.

On digital tape, a recording can be saturated in tape noise and distortion, with the playback system still being able to recover the data and deliver an almost faultless version of the original recording. In truth, the problems actually occur in the messy process of A/D and D/A conversion, as well as the rare occasions when the data has been corrupted and can't be correctly read.

If the sample frequency is much lower than the frequency of the original wave, an aliased output will be produced, resulting in dissonant harmonics.

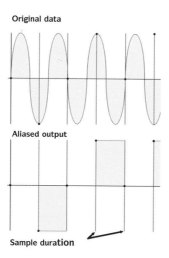

Original data

Aliased output

Sample duration

Are you converted?

As sound in its natural form is continuously variable, the task of transferring it into a stream of zeros and ones is a lot harder than you might imagine. One obvious problem is distortion – digital recording has a finite capacity, a number that cannot be exceeded at the top end of the digital scale. However, what happens beyond this point can vary

No clipping   **Saturate distortion**   **Digital bit overflow distortion**

from system to system. In older ADC chips, for example, the clipping results in digital bit overflow distortion – wrapping the samples around on themselves and placing the overs in the negative axis. Rather than just slicing the tops off the waveform (as with the more common saturate distortion), the clipping produces a radically different (and somewhat painful) waveshape.

Two different forms of digital clipping: saturate simply chops off the top of the waveshape, whereas digital bit overflow distortion wraps the waveshape around on itself.

At the other end of the scale, a recording with a wide dynamic range and plenty of quiet exposed sections can suffer from quantizing distortion, as the signal is squeezed into the remaining bits of the digital word. The solution to this is to record at high bit resolutions (24-bit, for example) or, when transferring to 16-bit, consider 'dithering down' your recording. Dithering adds small amounts of noise to effectively mask the effect of quantizing on lower-amplitude sounds, with several different manufacturers offering various optimised forms (Apogee's UV22, for example, or Logic Pro 7's POW-r).

Under another alias

If these first two considerations (distortion and quantizing) can be resolved by good engineering practice, the next set of errors relates to the quality and performance of your A/D converters. One area all converters struggle with is frequencies in the higher regions of the audio spectrum. As with the dynamics, any A/D converter has a finite response – in this case, to frequency; it simply can't sample the signal fast enough to capture the vibrations.

Nyquist's Theorem dictates that the sample frequency needs to be twice that of the upper bandwidth limit you need to record. In other words, at a sample rate of 44.1kHz, the highest frequency you can successfully capture is 22.05kHz.

Unfortunately, though, sampling at twice the bandwidth isn't quite enough to solve all the problems. If any signals in excess of the bandwidth limit enter the converter (in this case, 22.05kHz and above), the A/D conversion process will capture strange aliasing frequencies. These frequencies are caused by an inability to capture and represent the full wave cycle of the frequencies in question, creating dissonant extra harmonic material. The simple solution to this is to use an analogue filter – called an anti-aliasing filter – set at the bandwidth limit. But as we know, no analogue filter is perfect and a small slope (where some harmonics are let through) alongside phase shifts will degrade the performance.

As an alternative, oversampling converters work by sampling far in excess of the Nyquist limit and then using digital FIR filters (which are far steeper and more exact than their analogue counterparts) to shave off unwanted frequencies.

The jitters

To capture a bandwidth close to human hearing, an audio signal needs to be sampled thousands of times each second. The assumption would follow that the clock signal (or word clock) used to trigger this process is tight and unwavering, but this is often not the case. Poor-quality converters will suffer from a drifting clock generator, creating an effect known as jitter (the higher the jitter, the more unstable the clock). As jitter manifests itself as a discrete form of frequency modulation (FM), a poor-quality converter will end up creating unwanted high-frequency distortion and a lack of stability in the stereo image.

If a number of digital audio devices or converters are working together, the problem gets worse. For the devices to work simultaneously, they will all need to have their word clocks synchronised – in most cases, this means a number of slave devices will be daisychained to a master. As you'd expect, there's a high chance that your wordclock will now contain serious amounts of jitter, with the sound of your studio being largely dictated by the quality of word clock it's receiving. A professional-grade Masterclock generator – like Apogee's Big Ben – configured with star-based distribution provides a more acceptable solution, with almost immeasurably low jitter levels.

Correction centre

Assuming you've converted the signal, the biggest problem remaining is the integrity and readability of the data (especially in data-sensitive systems such as CD, DAT and ADAT, where the supply of audio information needs to be constant).

By contrast, a computer's hard drive can re-read the data until it interprets it correctly. Given that missing data sounds catastrophic, all these digital devices need some form of error detection and correction.

Interleaving the data can also prevent major data loss: the data is stored in a non-sequential, interleaved fashion and de-interleaved on playback. So, if a block of errors occurs, the damage will be distributed, rather than wiping out a number of consecutive samples.

As with any digital system, error detection involves a complex system of parity bits or CRC codes (cyclic redundancy checks) to calculate a checksum and flag up missing or problematic data. In other words, if the numbers don't add up, the playback engine knows that there's something wrong and where the problem is located. Where missing or corrupt data exists, the D/A converter can interpolate between the previous and next values – inserting a new value based on the average of those two points. The problem here, in respect to the signal integrity, is that error correction will largely happen without you knowing – or at least until the data becomes so corrupt that the error correction can't cope and the output descends into chaos.

A healthy respect

Given some good converters, a well-maintained recorder and the ability to work at resolutions like 24-bit/44.1kHz and above, there is no reason to expect that a recording will suffer or degrade significantly. Aspects like A/D conversion or word clock sync might not seem the most exciting aspects of

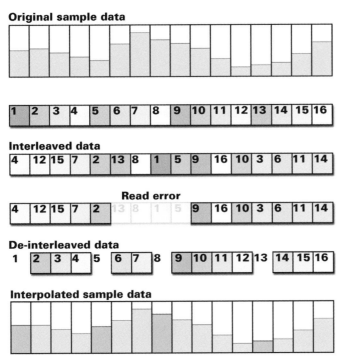

Original sample data

1 | 2 | 3 | 4 | 5 | 6 | 7 | 8 | 9 | 10 | 11 | 12 | 13 | 14 | 15 | 16

Interleaved data

4 | 12 | 15 | 7 | 2 | 13 | 8 | 1 | 5 | 9 | 16 | 10 | 3 | 6 | 11 | 14

Read error

4 | 12 | 15 | 7 | 2 | 13 | 8 | 1 | 5 | 9 | 16 | 10 | 3 | 6 | 11 | 14

De-interleaved data

1 | 2 | 3 | 4 | 5 | 6 | 7 | 8 | 9 | 10 | 11 | 12 | 13 | 14 | 15 | 16

Interpolated sample data

Digital recorders write data in an interleaved fashion. If any of the tape is corrupted, the damage discretely spreads, rather than producing obvious dropouts.

recording, but they are essential to getting the best from your digital studio. Equally, just because something is held in the digital domain doesn't mean that it's safe – we still need to be aware as to how signal degradation occurs.

Further info

For information on the fundamentals of digital audio, visit
www.teamcombooks.com/mp3handbook/11.htm
John Watkinson has written two authoritative books on digital audio:
Introduction to Digital Audio, ISBN 0-240-51643-5
Art of Digital Audio, ISBN 0-240-51587-0
For an insight into dithering, visit
www.apogeedigital.com/products/uv22hr.php

Tech terms

FIR filters
FIR filters use DSP calculations to produce a phase-linear frequency response. By contrast, an analogue filter produces small phase shifts, brought about by minute time differences between different frequencies.

Checksum
A checksum is a unique piece of code written alongside the original data and based on the sum of data it represents. On read or playback, if the checksum doesn't match the data, an error is reported.

Parity bit
A parity bit is a simple form of checksum that uses a single bit to identify the integrity of a bitstream. For example, a bitstream of 00110101 would have a parity bit value of 0 to indicate an even number of 1s in the bitstream.

Digital audio

Digitising audio is the process of converting sound into a series of numbers. The hardware that does the job is known, naturally enough, as an audio-to-digital converter, usually abbreviated to ADC. A digital-to-audio converter (DAC) reverses the process, converting digital audio in a sampler or on a hard drive, for example, to sound that we can hear.

The two most important aspects during conversion are the sample rate and the sample resolution, and these determine the overall quality of the material.

Sample rate

To convert sound to a digital format, the ADC measures or samples it a specified number of times per second. The more samples taken in a given time, the more accurate the digital representation of the sound. This can be seen clearly in Diagrams 1 and 2 below.

Diagram 1: This is clearly a sine wave, but you can see the steps in the waveform, showing the points at which it has been sampled.

Diagram 2: This sine wave has been recorded at a higher sample rate and is therefore more accurate and closer to the original waveform.

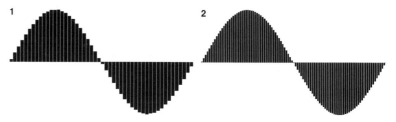

Although the second example is closer to a perfect sine wave, the steps are still evident, and on playback it might sound a little 'rough'. Diagrams 3 and 4 illustrate what happens at extremely high and low sample rates.

Diagram 3: This wave has been sampled at a very high sample rate and although the steps are there, we can see that it is virtually a pure sine wave.

Diagram 4: This wave has been sampled at a very low sample rate. The samples are so far apart that the sine wave is barely visible. On playback, it wouldn't sound like a sine wave.

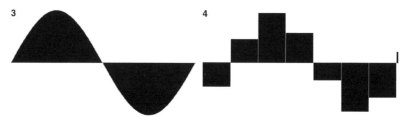

The Nyquist limit

So, we can clearly see that the higher the sample rate, the more accurate the digital representation of the sound. Mathematician Harry Nyquist showed that to accurately digitise a sound we only need to sample it at twice its frequency. Assuming the limit of human hearing is around 20kHz, we should be able to capture our full audio spectrum by sampling at 40kHz. So the 44.1kHz sample rate of audio CDs ought to give us a little headroom on that limit.

From Harry's calculations we get the Nyquist Limit, which is half the frequency of the sample rate. If you sample a frequency beyond the Nyquist Limit – that is, at more than half the sampling rate – the sample is 'folded over' and stored at a sampling rate value lower than it actually is. This creates an effect called aliasing, which produces frequencies that were not in the original recording, resulting in a distorted sound.

To prevent aliasing, most ADCs include a filter that removes frequencies above the Nyquist Limit. It's a steep filter (sometimes called a reconstruction or anti-aliasing filter) that tries to filter everything beyond the specified cut-off frequency. The filter is usually a part of the sampling hardware and not something a user is likely to have control over.

Another ADC hardware feature that helps maintain sound quality during recording is oversampling. As its name suggests, it samples the sound at a sample rate higher than the one specified and then resamples it down to the required rate. In soundcard specs you'll often see a line saying 32x, 64x or 128x oversampling.

You can also use oversampling on the way out – the digital-to-audio conversion – but that works in a slightly different way. It adds additional samples to those already present – a process called interpolation – in order to use a gentler filter. The process is quite complex and involved (see the For More Information box for a link to the gory details). Fortunately, again, this is done behind the scenes by the sampling system and requires no any user intervention. However, it's true to say that part of the quality of a sampling or hard disk recording system is down to the filters used in the hardware. And you usually get what you pay for.

The going rate

It will not have escaped your notice that many systems offer sample rates of 48kHz (although this is mainly for compatibility with DAT machines because 48kHz isn't that much of an improvement over 44.1kHz), with additional rates up to 96kHz, and some even go as high as 192kHz.

Are there advantages to using them? Actually, there's still some controversy over the benefits of these higher sampling rates. On the one hand, with the threshold of human hearing at 20kHz, why try to record anything higher? And from a practical viewpoint, many modern listeners play their music on mobile systems with headphones that are unable to appreciate even the quality of standard audio CDs.

The purists, on the other hand, argue that a 96kHz sample rate, for example, enables the accurate recording of frequencies at the upper threshold of human hearing and beyond. While one benefit is the prevention of aliasing, such frequencies may be difficult to notice on a purely objective level.

Tech terms

Dynamic range

This is the difference between the quietest and loudest parts of a signal, and the value is important when considering the number of bits in the sample resolution. The more bits, the greater the difference between the lowest and highest sample values.

Signal-to-noise ratio

Often abbreviated to SNR, it's the ratio between the level of the signal you're recording and the background noise inherent in the system. It's closely related to dynamic range because the greater the ratio, the wider the difference there can be between the quietest and loudest parts of a signal without noise getting in the way.

Decibel

Usually seen abbreviated to dB, this is technically a relative measure of the difference between two signals – which can be confusing. The most important thing to remember about decibel values is that a 6dB increase represents a doubling of the volume.

Although subjectively the psychoacoustic benefits can make the sound seem more open and airy, and give it more depth and space. The differences may be subtle, and you'll need both good ears and a good reproduction system to perceive a difference, but upon such subtleties hang the questions surrounding the benefits of modern digital audio recording.

Sample resolution

The sample resolution is the scale used to measure the recorded samples. Audio CDs use a sample resolution of 16 bits. Bits are binary numbers and are easily converted to decimal by raising 2 to the power of the bits. So 16 bits is 216, or 65,536. This is how many values there are to store the sampled data. And 8 bits will give us 28 or 256 values.

Returning for a moment to our sine wave, when we sample it, each value must be in the range of 0–65,536 for a 16-bit recording and in the range of 0–256 for an 8-bit recording. 16 bits, therefore, affords a much finer and more accurate representation of a sample than 8 bits.

Dynamic range

The ultimate goal in digital audio recording is to capture the full range of human hearing. The difference between the quietest and the loudest sounds we can hear is around 140dB. A 16-bit sample resolution gives us a maximum dynamic range of 96dB. (Tip: a quick way to calculate the dynamic range of a sample resolution is to multiply the number of bits by six.) That's pretty good and a massive improvement over 8-bit recording with a range of 48dB (8x6).

However, crank the resolution up to 24 bits and you get an ear-topping dynamic range of 144dB. Who could ask for more? Well, recording engineers for a start. Their problems with sample resolutions of 16 bits or below are due to a couple of issues called clipping and headroom.

Clipping and headroom

Let's say we're using 16 bits and along comes a sound that requires a value of 65,600. Working with a maximum dynamic range of 96dB this is quite likely. The resolution only enables values up to 65,336 so what happens? The sample is truncated, or clipped, and stuffed into the 65,536 box, resulting in distortion of the signal.

In practice, you try to get as much sound into the system as possible while recording, but to avoid unwanted clipping you may try to lower the overall sound level to give you some headroom. That may mean working with an effective resolution of just 14 or 15 bits, which in turn results in a reduction of dynamic range to 84dB or 90dB. And while that's much better than analogue tape, it doesn't fully realise the potential of 16 bits.

However, if you drop a few bits from a 24-bit recording, you still get a stupendous 132–138dB dynamic range, so you don't have to ride the input levels so carefully. Many consumer soundcards now support 24-bit recording. But up that to 32-bit, and you can afford a whole 8 bits of headroom, while still achieving the full dynamic range of human hearing. Just as 24-bit recording is now very affordable, one day all recording systems will support 32-bit.

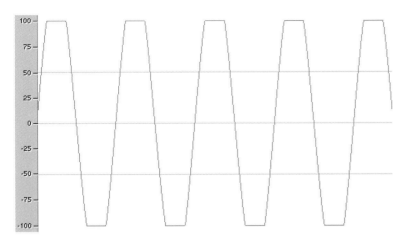

Clipping: If a waveform is clipped, it will have flat areas at its highest and lowest peaks.

One thing recording engineers who used to work with tape would do was to push the recording levels into the red. This caused a saturation effect on the tape, a little like compression, creating a warm sound. You simply can't do this with digital recording – all you'll do is clip – so don't even try it. There are lots of effects you can apply later to warm up the sound, if you feel it necessary.

Size matters

So after all that, it should be clear that higher sample rates and higher sample resolutions equal higher-quality audio. The major drawback of high-rated systems is that they require increased storage space and processing power. A 96kHz/24-bit recording, for example, requires three times more storage space than a 44.1kHz/16-bit recording.

In time, as computers continue to become more powerful, and hard disks grow larger, this won't be a consideration, but currently it is. You must, therefore, consider the trade-off between quality and storage space/processing power. If your system won't run to higher rates, remember that the humble audio-CD quality is still technically superior to the analogue reel-to-reel tape systems used on studio recordings until recently (though some audiophiles might dispute that fact). But if you're planning on upgrading your digital audio system, consider incorporating the higher rates and resolutions.

Further info

To delve into the more techy aspects of digital audio, visit
www.indiana.edu/~emusic/digital_audio.html
There's also a digital audio section at
www.earlevel.com
For information on oversampling, try
www.earlevel.com/Digital Audio/Oversampling.html
And perhaps we could direct you towards *The Quick Guide To Digital Audio Recording* available from www.pc-publishing.com

Envelopes

Our ears are amazing, and yet incongruous, organs. We can listen to a symphony orchestra and easily pick out individual instruments from within the acoustic mêlée – something no computer software has yet managed to do successfully and consistently – and yet they can easily be fooled by simple representations of complex acoustic sounds. Which is rather fortunate for us, otherwise the world of synthesis would be limited to drones and warbles, and totally unable to create any realistic sounds.

The ability to 'fool' the ear is particularly important for the third element of our synthesizer building blocks – volume shaping, which is performed by an envelope generator, also called a contour generator, a transient generator, or simply an ADSR – after the four phases it produces (Attack, Decay, Sustain and Release).

Just a phase

The main function of an envelope generator is to determine how the volume of a sound should change during its production (although it has other uses, too, which we'll look at later). A typical generator has four phases – Attack, Decay, Sustain and Release – which, between them, can mimic the sound envelopes of most acoustic instruments.

Note that three phases – Attack, Decay and Release – are a measurement of time, while Sustain is a volume level. So we talk about Attack, Decay and Release times, but a Sustain level. The envelope generator is normally triggered when a key is pressed on a synth keyboard and we can see how the phases fit together by relating them to a keypress.

Attack

This is the time it takes for the sound to reach a certain volume, usually the maximum volume. It begins as soon as you press a key or a note is triggered. Short Attack times are used for percussive sounds – such as drums, piano, guitar and so on – while longer Attack times would be used for strings, brass and a soft flute. Long Attack times are not found on acoustic instruments and tend to be used for electronic sounds and special effects.

Decay

The Decay phase starts as soon as the Attack phase ends. It's the time it takes the sound to fall from the level at the end of the Attack phase (normally its maximum level) to the Sustain level (which is normally lower than the volume the Attack phase hits) – we'll look at exceptions in a moment. For acoustic instruments, the Decay phase is usually longer than the Attack phase.

Sustain

This is the volume level the sound reaches at the end of the Decay phase. There is no specific time period attached to it; the Sustain volume ends when the key is released or the note ends.

Release

When the key is released, the envelope enters the Release phase, and this is the time it takes for the sound to die away to silence. Instruments such as a vibraphone and gong have long Release times. Note that, as its name suggests, the Release phase starts when the key is released. If the envelope is in the middle of its Attack or Decay phase at the point at which the key is released, the envelope jumps directly to the Release phase.

Four more or less

With just these four phases, it's possible to mimic most natural sounds and acoustic instruments – convincingly enough to fool our ears, in any case. However, not all sounds require all four phases. A wooden block, for example, simply has a fast Attack and fast Decay – the sound doesn't hang around long enough to enter a Sustain phase. This is a good illustration of the difference between the Decay and Release phases. The Decay phase kicks in immediately after the Attack phase, whereas you have to wait for the key to be released before the Release phase starts. The envelope of a wooden block is totally independent of the length of time the key is held down.

An electronic organ sound has no Decay phase. It hits maximum volume – the Sustain level – as soon as you press a key and stays there until you release the key, when it enters the Release phase.

The piano has a more complex envelope that must be constructed carefully. When you press a key the sound hits maximum volume almost immediately. If you hold your finger on the key, the sound dies away slowly; if you release the key, it dies away more quickly. There is no real Sustain phase. You need a fast Attack, a slow Decay, a faster Release and a zero Sustain level.

The importance of the envelope generator in determining how we perceive a sound should not be underestimated; it's every bit as important as the tone generator. To prove it, dial up a piano sound and then change the envelope to one you'd normally use for strings. It will sound odd. Likewise, apply a piano envelope to a string sound and it will probably sound a bit like a harpsichord.

For most acoustic sounds Attack, Decay and possibly Release times will be measured in milliseconds. However, in the world of synthesis the phases can be several seconds – or even minutes – long.

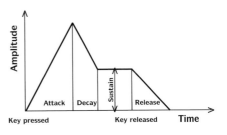

The four phases of a standard ADSR envelope are Attack, Decay, Sustain and Release.

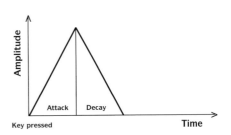

Some sounds, such as percussive sounds, only require an Attack and a Decay phase.

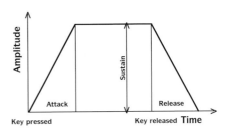

Sounds that are either completely on or off, such as an electronic organ, have no Decay phase.

IabmyC

A favourite sound among synthesists has long been the backwards cymbal, and this has enjoyed a new lease of life among Dance music practitioners. When a normal acoustic sound is produced, something is hit (a drum), stroked (a violin) or otherwise excited (the air inside a brass instrument) and the resulting sound is generated fairly quickly. In other words, it has a relatively fast Attack time. When such a sound ends, it always takes a little while for the sound to fade away completely, so there is always a short Decay or Release phase. These sorts of envelopes sound natural to us.

A backwards sound is unnatural because the sound builds up very slowly and then abruptly stops, with no Decay or Release phase. We can easily construct a backwards envelope by using a slow Attack time, with Decay and Release times of zero.

Breakpoints

ADSR envelopes were the norm with voltage-controlled analogue synthesisers, but there were variations, such as AD and ADR. As synthesis technology developed, it didn't take long before more complex envelopes were designed. One variation was to break some of the phases into two sections using what was called a Breakpoint, so you might find an ADBDSR envelope. This enables more complex and realistic envelopes to be constructed.

A Breakpoint is simply a point at which a change takes place, and Breakpoints are now commonly used in audio-editing software to enable you to draw a volume or pan envelope onto the signal. You can click Breakpoints onto the envelope line and drag the points to create virtually any envelope contour you wish.

As digital technology progressed, the multi-segment envelope appeared. This enabled you to specify both time and volume levels for each stage of the envelope. And as most processing was done in cheap software rather more expensive hardware, it was easy to dial up six, eight or more segments according to your desire for complexity. One feature of multi-segment envelopes is that they enable you to create a contour that rises, falls and then rises again in volume.

Envelopes and amplifiers

Whatever shape the envelope might be, you won't hear any sound at all until it's fed to an amplifier. The greater the envelope's amplitude during any phase, the more the amplifier opens, and the louder the sound will be.

Modular machinations

Although envelopes are primarily used to shape the volume of a sound, in a modular synthesizer you can connect it to other modules, too.

Let's assume we're using the archetypal ADSR envelope shown in the diagram at the top of page 53. What happens if you apply it to the cutoff control of a low-pass filter? If the cutoff in a low-pass filter is closed, all the sound will be filtered out. When the envelope opens, the cutoff shoots up creating a bright sound. Then it closes slightly during the Decay phase, dulling the

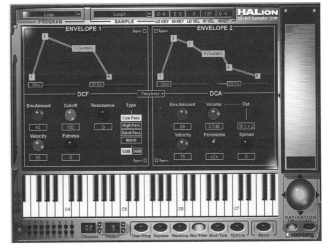

The envelope section of Arturia's Moog Modular V contains six envelope enerators, each with standard ADSR controls.

The envelope section in Steinberg's HALion soft sampler shows the phases clearly, making it easy to adjust them to your requirements.

sound, and it stays at that level until the Release period, when the sound gets less bright and finally fades away altogether.

We usually don't want an envelope to control the harmonics of a sound in such a severe way, so filters usually have a control to determine how much of the modulating signal is used. This is a useful technique because it's common for the harmonics of an acoustic instrument to change as its volume changes. Brass instruments, for example, generally become brighter as they are played louder.

You can also plug an envelope generator into an oscillator. You can probably work out what sort of pitch changes the envelope is likely to make to the oscillator's output. As with filters, an 'Amount' control will reduce the effect from a mad siren to a blip. It can be used to add the slight pitch lift that occurs at the start of many notes played on wind and brass instruments.

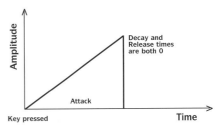

To create a 'backwards' sound you need a slow build-up to maximum volume and then an abrupt cut off.

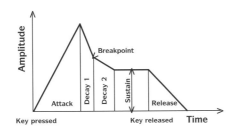

If you can add your own Breakpoints to an envelope you can create more complex envelopes.

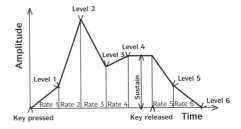

Digital technology gave rise to multi-segment envelopes where you can define a time and a volume level for each phase of the envelope.

14 EQ

Without any doubt, EQ is the most used – and abused – of all studio effects and it's an essential part of virtually all types of synthesis. That's because it works on a very important element of sound – the tone. In fact, at its simplest, all EQ does is cut and boost certain frequencies of sound. Think of a hi-fi's treble and bass controls – they're basic EQ controls. But, of course, technology has made EQ rather more sophisticated than that...

The good old days

EQ is short for Equalisation. In the good old days of recording – we're going back to 78s here – the recording process was significantly less sophisticated than it is today and it would typically lose the higher frequencies.

EQ was devised as a corrective process to boost the higher frequencies to compensate for this loss during the recording process to make the recorded sound 'equal' to the original. That's no longer the case with modern recording equipment and EQ is now used more as a creative effect.

No limit

The human range of hearing is typically quoted as running from 15Hz to 20kHz, although this varies considerably from individual to individual. In practice, it's generally not that wide, and we lose sensitivity to the upper frequencies with age and by listening to loud rock and dance music, so many people's upper limit may be closer to 15kHz.

You might expect this 'heard' range of frequencies to be those you'd be interested in EQ'ing. However, experiments have shown that frequencies above our normal range can affect our perception of the sound in subtle ways, so don't ignore them. For more about the basics of sound, take a look at the Ten Minute Master on Harmonics on page 84.

The combination of frequencies is what gives a sound its distinctive tone and when you Equalise a sound you boost and cut specific frequencies, which alters the tone.

In control

There are several controls typically used in filters and EQ effects:

- *Cutoff frequency/Cutoff point* The frequency at which a filter comes into play and starts to affect the sound. This determines which part of the frequency spectrum the filter works on.

Tech terms

Frequency response
The ear is more sensitive to some frequencies than others. Lower frequencies need to be louder than higher ones for us to perceive them as being at the same volume.

Fundamental
Generally the lowest (technically the first harmonic) and strongest frequency in a sound and the one that gives the sound its pitch.

Growl and Wha
If you apply a LFO (see the Ten Minute Master on Oscillators on page 100) to a filter it will vary the tone colour of the sound resulting in an effect called Growl. Controlled variations of the tone can produce a Wha effect.

EQ   57

- *Attenuation* The opposite of amplification, it reduces the target frequencies.
- *Level/Gain* A level or gain control enables you to cut (attenuate) or boost (amplify) a set of frequencies.
- *Bandwidth/Q/Resonance* The range of frequencies that will be affected by the filter either side of the cutoff point. Defined in Hertz, the terms 'bandwidth' and 'Q' are most commonly used in recording circles. Bandwidth is the more useful term because it describes exactly what the control does. Resonance is particularly common in synthesis. It boosts the frequencies around the cutoff point and can be used to put the filter into self-oscillation; not something you'd want to do in the recording environment.

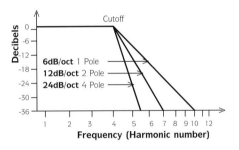

Resonance: In a low-pass filter of an analogue synthesizer, as the resonance is increased, it boosts the frequencies around the cutoff point.

Rolling around

There's one more factor to consider before looking at types of EQ and that's the rolloff curve or slope. This essentially describes how strong or severe a filter is. The steeper the slope, the more severe it is, and the greater the filtering effect as you move away from the cutoff point.

The rolloff is usually measured in decibels and the distance from the cutoff point is measured in octaves. A gentle filter, therefore, might have a rolloff of 6dB per octave, which means that for every octave away from the cutoff point, the signal is attenuated by 6dB. A filter with a 12dB per octave roll-off would be twice as strong and attenuate the signal by 12dB every octave.

Rolloff: The steeper a filter's slope or rolloff curve, the more quickly it attenuates the frequencies further away from the cutoff point. The steepest slope here is 24dB/octave.

Poles apart

In analogue synthesizers there are components within the filter circuits called poles, which apply an attenuation of around 6dB per octave. Some synthesizers use several poles and you may hear reference to a 1-pole, 2-pole, 3-pole or 4-pole filter. These would have a rolloff of 6dB/octave, 12dB/octave, 18dB/octave and 24dB/octave respectively. The more poles a filter has, the steeper the rolloff and the fewer frequencies will pass beyond the cutoff point. The famous Moog synthesizers were among the first to use 4-pole filters, which contributed to their 'fat' sound.

Not all synths tell you how many poles their filters have (or, in the case of digital synths and filters, how many poles they emulate) or let you change them (which ought to be easy in software). Lacking any precise information, you might assume a typical filter rolloff of 12dB/octave.

EQ types

There are a handful of common types of EQ and filters:

- *Fixed EQ* This is typically a single control such as Treble or Bass. A mixer might have Low (bass) and High (treble) EQ controls. The cutoff frequency here is fixed but you control the amount of cut or boost.

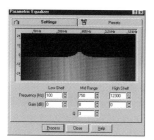

A parametric EQ with three adjustable frequency bands, gain controls and adjustable Q (bandwidth).

- *Graphic EQ* This divides the frequency range into a series of bands that you can cut and boost individually. They are easily recognised by a row of sliders, each controlling a specific frequency band. They are common on hi-fi systems, as standalone studio devices and can be found in software. Although you can technically divide the sound spectrum into any number of bands, typical numbers of divisions on hardware units are 15 and 31. Software developers are a law unto themselves and any number goes.
- *Parametric EQ* Whereas with a graphic EQ the frequency bands are fixed, parametric EQ enables you to change the frequency of the bands. Parametric EQs typically have three or four bands, each with three controls – cutoff frequency, bandwidth and level, enabling you to home in on specific frequencies within a very tight range.

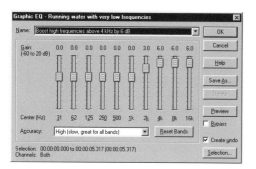

A software graphic EQ with ten bands, each twice the frequency of (and, therefore, one octave up from) the previous band.

- *Paragraphic EQ* This is a recent development born of the software revolution and it blurs the line between graphic and parametric. It typically offers several bands like a graphic, but with user-definable frequency bands like a parametric – it's a sort of super-parametric. However, as this can become quite complex, they also tend to have graphic interfaces so the user can see exactly which frequencies are being affected and by how much.
- *Sweeping/Semi-parametric* EQ A halfway house between fixed EQ and full parametric EQ; while the bandwidth is fixed, you can control the centre frequency (the cutoff point). It's common feature of many mixers. Typically you might find fixed Low and High EQ with a sweepable mid-range control.

Filter types

Somewhere within the gamut of filters, hovering between paras and graphics, there reside some popular filter types. They're easy to understand as they perform only one function. The first four are often, but not exclusively, found in synthesis, while the shelving filters are more commonly used in recording.

- *Low pass* This passes frequencies below the cutoff frequency and attenuates the higher ones. It is the most natural-sounding filter as higher frequencies are typically the first to be lost in natural environments.
- *High pass* This is the opposite of the low-pass filter; it passes frequencies above the cutoff frequency and attenuates lower ones. It's useful for removing unwanted bass frequencies and heavy use can remove the fundamental of a tone resulting in a very thin sound.
- *Band pass* As its name suggests, this passes a band of frequencies around the cutoff frequency and attenuates those either side. It's highly selective and particularly useful for homing in on specific frequencies such as tones produced by solo instruments or for tackling problem areas in a mix such as hum and noise. It is, in effect, a parametric EQ. Also known as 'peak' or 'bell' filters.

EQ   59

- *Band reject/Notch* This is the opposite of the band-pass filter. It attenuates frequencies either side of the cutoff frequency and passes the others, effectively notching out a frequency band.
- *High shelf* This usually boosts frequencies above the cutoff frequency. It's used as a tone control to shape the upper section of the frequency spectrum.
- *Low shelf* This is the opposite of the high-shelf filter and boosts frequencies below the cutoff frequency.

On the shelf

The terms 'high shelf' and 'high pass' are often used synonymously, as are 'low shelf' and 'low pass'. Technically, however, a high-shelf filter boosts frequencies above the cutoff point, whereas a high-pass filter simply passes them and attenuates the frequencies below. The net result may appear to be the same, but the resulting frequencies within the filtered sound will not be.

Having said that, modern shelving filters, particularly in software, can cut as well as boost, so cutting with a high-shelf filter is effectively the same as using a low-pass filter. It's just one of the ways in which modern technology blurs the lines.

Active and passive filtering

One final filter thing; you may occasionally hear some filter devices called 'active' or 'passive'. Passive simply means they can only attenuate frequencies, not boost them, much like low- and high-pass filters. Typical examples are a guitar's tone controls.

There are many EQ variants and it's important to know which ones do what. Learn this and you'll be better equipped to use them effectively in recording and synthesis.

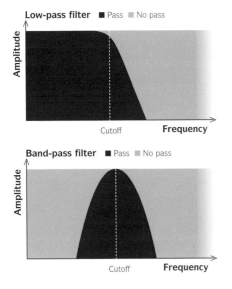

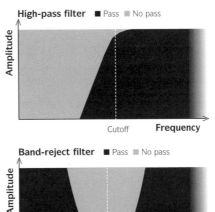

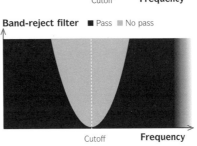

Common filter types: Low-pass and high-pass filters respectively pass frequencies below and above the cutoff point. Band-pass and band-reject filters respectively pass or reject frequencies either side of the cutoff point.

Exciters

For many of us, exploring the world of recording and mixing, we seem to be chasing an almost impossible ideal: vocals that jump out of a mix and demand the listener's attention, crisp percussion and acoustic guitar, earth-rumbling bass lines and so on. In an effort to achieve these qualities, an engineer's first choice of sonic weaponry is often the EQ unit, to accentuate that 'must-have' characteristic of any given sound. But all too often in these sit-

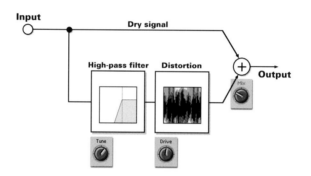

A simple schematic of an exciter – note the three principal controls (Tune, Drive and Mix) and their relation to the signal path.

Behringer's Ultrafex adds valve technology to the excitement process. This makes a lot of sense, as the extra harmonic information created by the valves contributes additional body and sparkle, even with the exciter bypassed.

uations, EQ doesn't deliver quite the right results – its effect being to highlight weaknesses in the original recording rather than to add weight or sparkle. Ultimately, an EQ has to deal with the material it's presented with – it can't add harmonic material, it can only re-balance it.

By contrast, exciters work in an additive way, adding extra harmonic information to make a sound appear bigger, brighter and more up-front in varying amounts. Unlike EQ, the ease with which you can add treble and tighten the bass without any great effort make exciters a desirable (and dangerous!) audio tool: once you've tasted the delights of an exciter, it's hard to resist applying increasingly large amounts! Enhancers – a variation on the exciter theme –

BBE's Sonic Maximizer provides a more subtle form of enhancement, best suited to full-spectrum recordings. Its approach focuses on phase anomalies between bass and treble transients.

offer similar results through careful manipulation of phase characteristics and some additional dynamic equalisation. But with so much secrecy surrounding the processes involved, how do you differentiate between the different approaches and techniques of exciters and enhancers?

The original – and arguably the best – form of exciter, as made by Aphex. The Aural Exciter works well with dull material needing a significant treble boost.

An exciting beginning

The origins of enhancement – in its broadest sense – date back to the mid-70s and the birth of Aphex Systems. The company's original product, the Aural Exciter, was discovered almost by accident when Aphex's co-founders, Marvin Caesar and Curt Knoppel, noticed some unusual signals emitting from a faulty valve amplifier. Refining the technology into a finished product, Caesar and Knoppel soon realised they had something hot on their hands, with many producers clamouring to make use of the Aural Exciter's unique abilities. At first the Aural Exciter was available only on a rental basis ($30, in 1975 prices, per finished minute of recorded time), possibly as a means of keeping the processes and technology relatively secret. Even so, the Aural Exciter soon became a must-have processor for any mixing or mastering session.

Later versions of the Aural Exciter – types B and C – saw the product released into the public domain, and Aphex continue to refine aural excitement with its current products: the 204 Aural Exciter/Big Bottom and Xciter guitar pedals. Recognising the potential for enhancers and exciters, other manufacturers developed similar systems, including BBE's Sonic Maximizer, Behringer's Ultrafex and SPL's Vitalizer, alongside a number of similar plug-in versions.

The joys of treble and bass

Our perception of bass and treble is fundamental to an understanding of the principles of exciters and enhancers – and go a long way to explaining the continuing popularity of these techniques. Our enjoyment of recorded music is deeply rooted in the amount and amplitude of bass and treble present – you only have to look at the number of stereo systems with their tone controls turned fully up to realise this! Understanding the psychoacoustics behind this isn't rocket science: as music gets louder we hear proportionally more treble and bass in comparison to middle frequencies – our ears, therefore, perceive the tone-boosted hi-fi as louder, even if it's played at the same volume as a more 'balanced' system.

Given our enjoyment of the extremes of the audio spectrum, making a recording that includes prominent amounts of both treble and bass is crucial to its success. Also, as many recordings will be played back at much lower volumes than their real-life equivalents, it is often desirable to enhance treble and bass levels to approximate the experience of listening at high volumes. Careful enhancement, rather than over-processed equalisation, helps retain and augment the life, presence and excitement of a recording – qualities that we, as listeners, specifically relate to the harmonic content of the track in question.

Creating the harmonics

So, having established treble and bass as being desirable qualities, how does an exciter go about creating a bigger, brighter sound? The addition of new upper harmonics (treble), is technically straightforward – just add some gentle distortion to see a corresponding rise in frequency content. What is a little more difficult, however, is adding harmonics in a way that doesn't produce nasty intermodulate distortion or unwanted harshness. The solution, as demonstrated in the principles behind the Aphex Aural Exciter, is to insert a high-pass filter ahead of the distortion, and carefully mix the dry and distorted signals together. The output of the Aural Exciter retains a natural mid range, but gains a more excited, slightly distorted top end.

Looking at the controls of an Aural Exciter, the technique can be seen in action. A Drive parameter (sometimes also known as Harmonics) creates the distortion; pushing this harder creates more distortion – and more harmonics. The Tune parameter corresponds to the high-pass filter, setting the cutoff point for frequencies filtered ahead of the distortion. Ideally, Tune should be kept reasonably high to avoid distorting the body of the track, but low enough to catch the top harmonics of the input. Finally, a Mix control balances the distorted signal with the output, with the desired result hopefully sounding enhanced, but not obviously distorted.

Sub-harmonic synthesis

In the task of adding bass energy, distortion is not an effective option, as the added harmonic information is generally higher than the fundamental frequency (rather than lower). Creating a deeper, more refined bass image is therefore problematic, but some strategies exist. Sub-harmonic synthesis is one such option: in this process, the signal is analysed and a new bass synthesised and added an octave below the original material. The technique is popular with bass guitarists, who can often be seen using octave-divider footpedals. Recent advances – as evident in Peavey's Kosmos and Logic Pro's SubBass – have seen big improvements in the tracking technology manufacturers are employing, as previously this technique was limited to simple monophonic input.

A comparison of a transient processed with (above) and without (below) the BBE Sonic Maximizer. Note the resultant poorly defined transient outputted by the loudspeaker on the unprocessed version.

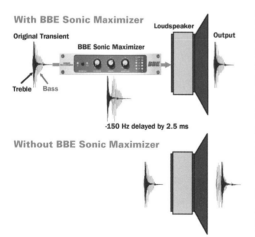

Not surprisingly, the output of sub-harmonic synthesis is quite literally earthshaking, especially on systems with proper sub-bass monitoring. But there is a fundamental problem inherent in the technique, particularly when applied wholesale across an entire mix. Unlike treble, bass takes up the significant proportion of a track's total sound energy levels – notice how the kick drum and bass, rather than the hi-hats, define a track's overall level. Therefore, adding extra sub-harmonic bass could have significant repercussions on your track's overall sound level, effectively forcing you to turn the whole mix down.

A transient phase

An alternative approach to bass enhancement – and, indeed, enhancement in general – is to take a closer look at the phase characteristics of treble and bass in conjunction with our perception of transient detail. Transients – the initial bursts of sound energy at the start of a note – form a vital role in defining the energy and detail of a track. Ideally, it is important that both the treble component and bass component of a transient are aligned in perfect phase – but sometimes this not the case. The main culprit in this situation is the loudspeaker itself: although its overall amplitude response is good (that is, how quickly the speaker reacts to its input), the phase response between low and high frequencies isn't entirely synchronous.

With these observations in mind, the BBE Sonic Maximizer seeks to restore discrepancies between the phase alignment of bass and treble transients – effectively delaying the bass by a few milliseconds to mirror a speaker's sluggish treble output. Additional dynamic equalisation – program-dependent sweetening of the treble and bass through expansion and compression – provides additional clarity and polish. In use, the restored transient detail created by the BBE process adds tightness and a more up-front quality to recordings, making the sound appear much closer to its original acoustic form. Big Bottom, the bass end of the Aural Excitement process, uses similar phase shifting and dynamic equalisation to create a tighter bass without unnecessarily high signal levels.

Too much of a good thing?

The key to using any enhancer successfully – albeit an Aural Exciter, Sonic Maximizer or equivalent – is moderation. As with excessive equalisation, the ear can quickly become tuned to the result, so remember to make detailed comparisons of the signal before and after processing. Like many other facets of life and sound engineering, over-indulgence and exposure can be fatiguing – keep a perspective on what you're trying to achieve and reserve the 'treat' of an exciter/enhancer for those special moments when nothing else will do. Clearly, there are also inherent differences in the principles of enhancing and exciting that make each one better suited to certain situations. If the material is well-presented, turn to a phase-shifting enhancer; if your top end is dull (or non-existent) an exciter may be the best option. Either way, you can expect your sound or mix to be presented with all the clarity and definition it deserves.

More tech terms

Dynamic equalisation

Dynamic equalisation – in the context of exciters and enhancers – refers to the use of compression and expansion to change the spectral balance of a given sound. If an audio input is split into two bands, with the lower band compressed, the perception of bass will increase without any increase in the overall sound levels.

Sub-harmonics

Sub-harmonics are harmonics beneath the fundamental frequency, or pitch, of a note. The most musical sub-harmonic is an octave below the fundamental and is often seen as a sub-oscillator on many synthesizers.

Further info

To find out more about the process and techniques mentioned:
www.bbesound.com
www.aphex.com
www.peavey.com/products/kosmos
To understand more about our enjoyment and perception of frequency visit:
www.wordiq.com/definition/ Psychoacoustics
arts.ucsc.edu/ems/music/tech_background/TE-03/teces_03.html
For more information on sub-harmonics visit:
www.yogimont.net/jia/roughness

Fades and crossfades

There's more to a good fade than meets the eye (...or ear). Fades are used at both the macro (recording) and micro (sample) level. Creating fades and crossfades, at both the recording and sample levels, requires a little application. It's a creative part of audio editing, and a technical understanding of the process will help you do a better job. We'll look at the considerations involved when working at both these levels in this feature. But first, let's get some terminology out of the way...

A fade is a gradual increase or decrease in volume. In recording it's most commonly used to fade out a song. In fact, fade-out endings for songs have become almost de rigueur, giving rise to the premise that songwriters are no longer able to write proper endings for their songs...

The fade-out has not always been a song-writing device. Paul Anka's chart-topping Diana back in 1957 was widely claimed to be the first pop song to use a fade, but we reckon it wasn't, and there are several earlier fade-outs including The Charms' Hearts of Stone from 1955.

Fade away

Anyway, if you want to do a fade, do it right. Decide if you want a short fade or a long fade and make sure there's enough material for the fade. With modern sequencers, it's easy enough to copy the chorus, or the last few phrases, to the end of the song, giving you plenty of material to work with.

The most intuitive way to fade is to use the faders on a mixer, of either the hardware or software variety. All modern software sequencers will record your movements so you can fade, tweak and edit until you get it just right.

There is usually an optimum point for the fade to actually fade to nothing. You'll hear this instinctively if you listen to fade-outs. In most cases, it's at the end of the chorus or phrase. In other words, the song ends at a natural end point. This isn't always the case, but it's a good place to start – or end – when creating your own fades.

Choose your curve

The alternative to performing a manual mix is to create a master audio file of the song and either apply an editor's fade function, or draw a fade onto it with a volume envelope, again both standard fare in modern sequencers and audio editors.

Fade functions often give you a choice of fade curves. The two most common types are linear and logarithmic. Linear fades are simply straight lines, whereas

A logarithmic fade may sound more natural than a linear fade as our hearing responds logarithmically.

A linear fade is easy to apply, and with software you can specify the exact start and end points.

logarithmic fades are curves. Our ears respond to volume in a logarithmic way, so log fades may seem to be the most natural. And in many cases they are, but don't dismiss a linear curve until you've tried it; sound, music and mixing are as much art as science.

Drawing in a curve gives you more control, although it can be easy to get carried away if you stray too far from a linear fade, and log fades are not easy to draw by hand. But drawing is useful if you don't want to fade in a regular manner.

The reason that manual mixing often produces the best fades is that we mix what we hear, so considerations about linear and log curves don't come into the

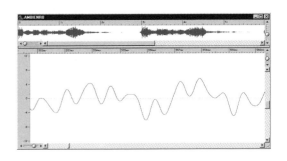

If you zoom in on a waveform, what you'll see is a wavy line oscillating above and below the horizontal zero-crossing point.

equation. Also, you might not fade in a regular way. For example, on each repeat you may decide to fade the start of the chorus less and then fade faster halfway through. This may be easier to do manually than by drawing. Whatever method you decide to use, some experimentation will undoubtedly be necessary.

Not fade away

Considerably less popular with songwriters and producers than the fade-out is the fade-in. However, this very fact can be used to make a song a little different. Fade-ins work exactly like fade-outs – but in reverse, of course. In most cases, it's a good idea to keep a fade-in short unless you're after a particular effect. The fade function in a sequencer or audio editor can often be used here very quickly and effectively.

Crossfades

Unlike a fade, which is performed on one piece of audio, a crossfade requires two pieces of audio, and is the process of fading one out while simultaneously fading the other one in. In recording, this is primarily used to make one track on an album fade or merge into the following one. When done successfully, it's a great effect.

As with fades, you can perform a crossfade manually. You need mixed versions of the two songs routed to two different sets of faders. The two songs must be on different tracks, and the end of the first song must overlap the start of the second. As with fades, make sure there's enough overlapping material to do the crossfade you want to do.

Ways to fade

There are several ways to do a crossfade. The most obvious is to fade the first track out at a uniform rate, while simultaneously fading in the second. However, you might want to fade the first out for a short while before fading in the second. Or you might want to fade up the second track, so that it's bubbling under the first one, before fading out the first. Unless you're after a special effect, use the first method.

Performing a crossfade is a little more involved than doing a fade, so it's worth looking at the help you can get from your sequencer or audio editor. Most have a crossfade function and, again, some offer a choice of curves. You may also be able to use one curve for the fade-out and a different one for the fade-in.

Loopmasters

The principles of crossfading are nowhere more essential than in sample and loop editing and creation. Being able to crossfade well is the mark of a polished loop maker. Whereas our ears can be quite forgiving if two songs are crossfaded in a slipshod way, if you don't get the crossfade in a loop or sample right, there will be a very noticeable click.

Software can help, of course, and you'd be ill-advised to try looping without some soft assistance. There are a few experienced loopers who profess to do it by ear and touch, but why make life difficult?

Level crossings

The secret of a good loop is to find zero-crossing points in the sample. If you zoom in closely on a waveform, you'll see it as a wavy line that oscillates above and below a central horizontal line. When the waveform is on the horizontal line, it is at zero volume, and these are the places where you need to cut the sample. Most audio editors have a function that automatically cuts the audio at zero-crossing points to help make seamless joins.

If you cut audio when the waveform is above or below the line, the waveform will be at a certain level. If you butt this break against a waveform, unless their levels match exactly, you'll hear a click or glitch. Many pieces of software have a Loop Tuner or a Loop Finder, which butts the end of the sample up against the start of it, so you can see and hear what it will be like when looped. These make loop creation so much easier.

WaveLab's Crossfade Looper puts the end of a loop up against the start and enables you to jiggle the two sections until they make a good fit.

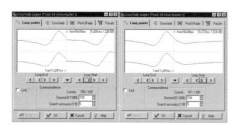

Shape of fades to come

When making loops, it's not always enough simply to cut at zero-crossing points. You should also look at the shape of the wave and try to pick points so that the join looks like a continuation of the waveform. So, for example, if the waveform leading to the zero-crossing point at the end of the loop sweeps up from below the line, look for the waveform in the next section to continue the curve above the line.

Also, for a seamless loop, the tone at the start and end needs to be similar. You won't find it easy to fade the end of a piano sample into the start of a trumpet sample. Actually, there are ways to do this...

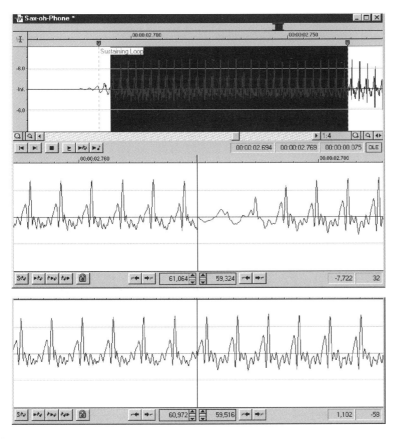

Sound Forge's Loop Tuner: The butt point in the sample in the top picture is not at all smooth. In the lower example the start and end points have been shuffled to create a smooth, flowing waveform.

Cut tips

If you have a stubborn sample or want to loop a sample with different start and end sounds, try this. Copy a section from the start of the sample and merge it with the end. Use your editor's merge function or do it with a crossfade. This adds part of the tone from the start of the sample, to the end – which should make it easier to loop.

If you are creating your own samples for looping, here's another tip. Instead of recording the sample just once, record it twice in succession and make the loop from the second recording. This allows any frequencies at the end of the first sample – any reverb tails, for example – to be captured at the start of the second sample, so the start and end of the sample are more likely to have a similar sound. It's the same kind of idea as the previous tip.

Further info

For an excellent discussion about using software curves, visit
www.editorsguild.com/newsletter/ SepOct99/tipaudio_cross.html

A feature on making orchestral samples sound more real, and a discussion of sample crossfading techniques
www.soniccontrol.com/tech/midi/ articles/010100/feature.shtml

Tech terms

Butt splice
This is the alternative to a crossfade, where two pieces of audio are simply stuck next to each other. This was a typical join in the days of tape recording, but with modern software there's no excuse for sloppy butting.

Transition
The movement from one state to another, typically used to describe a crossfade (and sometimes used as a verb by those who know no better).

Glitch
A click or some other disruption in the playback. Audio edits, such as loop-making, can easily create a glitch if there's a difference between the amplitudes of the two sections of audio that are joined together.

Filters

Ask any synthesist where the true character and muscle of any synthesizer lies and there will only ever be one answer – its filters. All the great synthesizers of our time (the Minimoogs, Prophets and TB-303's of this world) can attribute a large part of their success to the characteristic sound of their filters. Ultimately the sound of electronic music is the sound of the filter ripping, screeching, roaring, murmuring or growling its way through the audio spectrum.

We've never had so many filtering devices to choose from as we have today – from hardware devices re-creating the sounds of old, through to the very latest software plug-ins pushing new sonic boundaries. Equally, the range of filters has grown far beyond the simple, but classic, low-pass option. Many current synthesizers and samplers include an array of filtering options that include band-pass, high-pass, band-reject, notch and peaking filters.

Faced with such a bewildering choice, making the right decision can be daunting. But armed with a more informed understanding of the working principles of filters, you can start making more confident choices and expand your sound repertoire accordingly.

Filter essentials

Subtractive synthesis, which we touched on in the Ten Minute Master on analogue synthesis (page 1), works on the principle of removing certain harmonics from harmonically rich material, such as pulse or sawtooth waveforms. Different filters remove different elements, thus producing different end results. Filters are easily the most important and exciting element of any subtractive synthesizer, turning a few simple wave shapes into a plethora of contrasting sounds and timbres.

Band-pass and notch filters are created by routing low-pass and high-pass filters in series or parallel configurations.

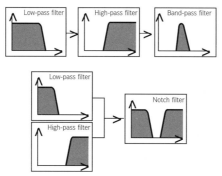

A good starting point for looking at filters in more detail is the low-pass filter. This is the most commonly implemented filter type, and easily the most useful on a day-to-day basis. The principle parameter involved in a low-pass filter, or indeed any other filter is the Cutoff Point. Above this point frequencies, or harmonics, will begin to be attenuated, while lower frequencies will be permitted to pass – hence the term 'low pass'.

The result of filtering is a change in the sound's timbre – from the initial bright sound of an open filter to a progressively darker version with fewer higher harmonics as the filter closes. Looked at with an oscilloscope, a saw-tooth wave will begin to become increasingly rounded and closer to the shape of a sine wave as this process happens. In theory, with a strong enough filter, a sawtooth wave could be filtered right down to a sine wave – removing all the harmonics to leave just the single fundamental frequency.

Muscle power

One of the major differences between the sound of different manufacturer's filters lies in their relative strengths. Theoretically speaking, a perfect filter would have no frequencies evident above the cutoff point. However, this is not the case with a traditional analogue filter. As the low-pass filter diagram illustrates, the actual cutoff is far from being a straight line – so some frequencies above the cutoff point do pass through, although at progressively attenuated amplitudes. Certain filter designs are more effective than others, with the strength being measured in dB (per octave) or 'poles'. Essentially, the higher the pole count (or dB rating), the steeper the cutoff attenuation and the more powerful the filter.

Probably one of the many reasons why Minimoog filters were so highly revered was for their power (24dB, or 4-pole), compared to the weaker filters (12dB, or 2-pole) of many of the cheaper Japanese synths. That said, weaker filters are supposed to sound more natural than their stronger, more synthetic counterparts, so it's debatable what is actually 'best'. Thankfully, on today's multimode filters, different pole settings are increasingly a standard feature, with some synths going as far as 6- or even 8-pole.

For real analogue purists, synthesizers like the ATC-1 (Analogue Tone Chameleon) actually include different filter cartridges that effectively re-create the differences between different filter designs. Also, many current manufacturers of modular synths (Doepfer, Analogue Solutions) include different filter modules built from the original (and sometimes flawed) designs of their vintage synthesizer forebears.

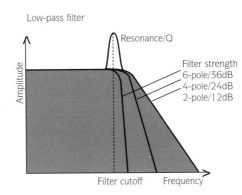

The familiar response curve of a low-pass filter, including variable pole settings and the characteristic effect of resonance.

Getting dirty

Harder to discern, but equally part of the filter's character, are phasing inconsistencies, and that old bugbear of equipment design – distortion. Ironically, the things that many designers seek to eliminate are the very characteristics that we, as musicians and engineers, seem to revel in – and distortion in fil-

With 14 filters types, four filters per patch and a Waveshaper module, Absynth is a good choice for getting your teeth into filtering.

ters is no exception. Realising this fact, many manufacturers now incorporate and exploit some element of distortion to 'grit up' the sound. Theoretically this makes perfect sense, as the process of distortion will add more harmonic material for the filter to play with.

Take a closer look at devices like the Sherman Filterbank, or Waldorf's very desirable (but not exactly low cost) AFB16 (Analogue Filter Bank 16) to see distortion deliberately being incorporated into analogue filters. Another type of distortion often included with (or alongside) a filter, is waveshaping. Native Instruments' Absynth includes a waveshaper module between its two filters, while Waldorf's Microwave XT includes a fantastically gritty waveshaping filter.

It resonates

If you choose to feed back some of the filter's output to itself, the filter's circuit will begin to resonate, so creating the characteristic sound of resonance. Looking again at the low-pass filter curve diagram, this will be seen as the peak around the cutoff frequency, which will boost any harmonics present. Pushed even further, a good filter will also begin to self-oscillate, creating a new fundamental at a pitch equal to the cutoff frequency.

Resonance is a highly desirable effect, making even the slightest modulation of the filter cutoff all that more noticeable. The result of resonance is also dependant on the level of the cutoff. A high cutoff tends to make sounds thinner and more nasal, while a low cutoff will increase the bass end. There are also major differences between the resonances of different manufacturer's filters, varying between the liquid squeals of a 303 to the more refined and powerful sound of Moog resonance.

Beyond the low-pass filter

Although the range of a good low-pass filter enables the creation of a range of timbres, the boundaries can be pushed even further by employing other filter types. High-pass filters work in much the same way as their low-pass siblings, but in reverse. In this case, frequencies below the cutoff point are attenuated, with the higher frequencies and harmonics being allowed to pass untouched. The result is a thinner, brighter sound as the cutoff point is raised. This filter offers a good contrast to the low-end weight of a low-pass filter and is a useful tool for removing mix-cluttering, lower-mid frequencies.

It's possible to create band-pass and notch filters by combining low-pass and high-pass filters. To construct a band-pass filter, the high- and low-pass filters are connected in series – the sound flowing first through the low-pass filter to remove high frequencies, and then on to the high-pass filter to remove bass frequencies. The end result of this process is a narrow bandwidth of frequencies being allowed to pass and a sound that is deep and dark, or thin and bright, at the two extremes of cutoff position.

By connecting a high-pass and low-pass filter in parallel, a notch filter (also known as band reject) is created. In this case, the sound passes through each filter separately and is then summed to form the output. The net result of this is an attenuation of frequencies around the cutoff point, not entirely dissimilar to notching out frequencies on a graphic equaliser. Where both these filter types excel is their ability to hone in on, and work with, very specific harmonics, either removing them (in the case of the notch filter) or accentuating them (in the case of the band-pass filter).

Another twist on the band-pass/band-reject theme is the peaking filter, which boosts frequencies at the cutoff point while allowing the rest of the frequency range to pass relatively untouched. To some extent, the peaking filter is less akin to filtering (which removes harmonics) and much closer to EQ (which cuts or boosts harmonics), but is often included as an option in the filter.

Advanced techniques

As you can begin to see, from just a few simple filter types combined in various ways, a whole range of sonic possibilities can be explored. Programs such as Reaktor 4 and Tassman 3 enable you to patch your own filter configurations to explore these techniques. Antares' new Filter plug-in is also a good example of the possibilities offered by combining four multimode filters alongside some interesting and dynamic modulation sources – step sequencers, envelopes, and so on.

Many advanced synthesis techniques make use of multiple band-pass filters, one such example being 'formant synthesis'. Formant synthesis originated from research into synthesising the human voice. Viewed on a spectral analyser, the spectral envelope of the voice can be seen as a series of peaks and troughs. This can be easily recreated using multiple (parallel) band-pass filters set to specific frequencies. The Emu Emulator 4 series included a particularly comprehensive range of filters (21 at the last count), including some interesting Z-plane formant filters used to morph between vowel sounds. More recent soft synths, such as the VirSyn Cube, include options to create your own unique filter response curves for formant synthesis.

Further info

Access-Music commissioned an informative programming tutorial guide for Virus synths, although it's useful for any budding synthesist. A downloadable PDF of this can be found in its news archives at:
www.access-music.de/news.php4
For more information on Waldorf's AFB 16 and range of synthesizers visit:
www.waldorf-gmbh.de
Examples of modular synthesizer modules, including some very interesting analogue filters can be found at
www.doepfer.de
The man who pioneered it all is Bob Moog
www.moogmusic.com
A comprehensive overview of almost any synth you could care to mention, or own
www.vintagesynth.org

Tech terms

Harmonics
A sound's timbre (tone colour) is the sum of a series of harmonics at different frequencies and amplitudes. Different wave shapes (sawtooth, square etc.) can be defined by the amount and density of these harmonics.

Spectral analysis
A plot of a sound's timbre, including the frequency and amplitude of the fundamental, alongside its associated harmonics.

Z-plane
A type of filter that can change its function over time. This usually involves creating two filter configurations and morphing between the two setups.

Formant
A number of characteristic fixed resonant peaks in the spectral response of the human voice. The alignment and amplitude of these peaks creates the different vowel sounds crucial to speech.

FireWire

It's all about the need for speed. As computer technology has developed we've seen a startling array of communications protocols (not to mention acronyms) – IDE, EIDE, ISA, PCI, AGP ADB, SCSI, USB and so on. Some have specialist uses – AGP for graphics cards and IDE for hard disks, for example – while others, such as SCSI and USB, are designed for a range of devices – from hard disks and scanners to mice and keyboards.

FireWire is one of the most recent communications protocols to arrive (although it has now been around for several years). However, it's only in the last year or so that it's been used for MIDI and audio interfaces. Its purpose is quite simple; to transfer data from one device to another – as much of it as possible and as quickly as possible.

Say cheese

FireWire's first area of application was DV – Digital Video. It was heavily promoted by Apple a few years ago when Steve Jobs, Apple's CEO, was pushing DV as if MGM was going out of business.

DV didn't turn us all into Spielbergs, but it did give would-be Tarentinos the opportunity to turn out terrible movies for next to nothing. Perhaps more importantly, it also enhanced awareness of the protocol, which led manufacturers to produce all manner of other FireWire devices – disk drives, scanners, CD-R drives and printers.

Origin of the species

The origin of FireWire goes back to 1986. It's commonly considered to be an Apple development, although some sources attribute it to an inter-company development group, the brief of which was to develop a superior serial bus. Wherever the original idea came from, there's no doubt that Apple picked up the ball and ran with it. It was standardised in 1995 with the official name of IEEE-1394.

In true Apple style, interest in FireWire was forced upon Mac users. Macs had traditionally used SCSI as a hard drive interface because it was faster than the PC's IDE protocol. But in a cost-cutting exercise, Apple threw SCSI out the window – along with the Macintosh serial and parallel ports – and in went IDE drives, and USB and FireWire interfaces. Mac users had to ditch old devices and buy new ones – or convert to the PC, which many did. But the demand for FireWire and USB devices spurred developers into making prod-

FireWire 400's six-core wire, showing the two wires that can carry up to 45W of power to peripherals.

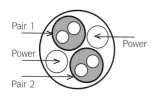

MOTU's UltraLite bus-powered FireWire audio interface delivers everything you need to turn your laptop or desktop Mac or PC into a mobile 24-bit, 96kHz recording studio with 10 inputs and 14 outputs

ucts that ultimately pushed PC manufacturers into taking up USB and FireWire on the PC, too.

Then there's iLink…

As we've said, FireWire's first mainstream use was for video, and when it was being added to almost all DV camcorders other companies happily slapped their own moniker on it. Hence we have Sony's iLink, which is essentially the same protocol. However, iLink only uses four wires, not FireWire's six. The two missing wires are used to carry power in FireWire, so iLink needs to be used with devices which have their own power supply.

Let's count the ways…

The benefits of FireWire over other communications protocols are many, so let's take a look at its main features.

- Fast data transfer Typically, this has been 400Mbps (megabits per second), implemented by Apple as FireWire 400, but FireWire 800 is now available, which runs at 800Mbps, and FireWire can go even faster than that, as we'll see in a moment.
- Hot-pluggable with Plug and Play connectivity This means you can connect and disconnect FireWire devices without switching off your computer. There are no device IDs to assign or terminators to connect, as there is with SCSI.
- Combined Asynchronous and Isochronous transfer For guaranteed data delivery (see the Tech Terms box).
- Up to 63 FireWire devices can be used at the same time Devices can be connected in a chain or via FireWire hubs.
- Peer-to-peer technology Using a hub, this enables several computers and peripherals to be connected at the same time.
- Low cost The FireWire interface is relatively inexpensive compared to SCSI, for example.
- Low-cost cables Again, standard cables are less expensive than SCSI cables.
- Long cable runs FireWire 400 supports traditional cable runs of up to 4.5 metres. However, with optical cable, runs of up to 100 metres are supported.

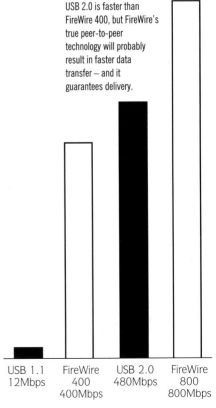

USB 2.0 is faster than FireWire 400, but FireWire's true peer-to-peer technology will probably result in faster data transfer – and it guarantees delivery.

| USB 1.1 12Mbps | FireWire 400 400Mbps | USB 2.0 480Mbps | FireWire 800 800Mbps |

- Power supplied Power can be supplied to FireWire devices via the FireWire cable.
- Networking Computers can be networked via FireWire using standard networking protocols. FireWire 400 is faster than 100 BASE-T, the most common Ethernet connection, while FireWire 800 is almost as fast as 1000 BASE-T.

If you compare these features with FireWire's two main competitors – USB and SCSI – you'll see that FireWire wins out in virtually every area.

What about USB 2.0?

The original USB protocol, now USB 1.1, was intended to do little more than connect mice and keyboards, so its data transfer rate wasn't really a major issue. However, some enterprising developers tried developing USB hard drives, which really pushed the limits of its capabilities given its transfer rate of 12Mbps.

So USB 2.0 was developed, which offers a massive 480Mbps throughput. However, there are differences between USB 2.0 and FireWire that make FireWire the preferred choice for digital audio and video applications.

For example, FireWire is a true peer-to-peer technology, while USB uses a master/slave relationship. This means that to transfer data from one USB device to another, it must be copied to a central computer and back again. Two FireWire devices can send data directly to each other without a middle-man, so FireWire 400 could still prove to be faster than USB 2.0's 480Mbps – and that's without taking into account the faster speed of FireWire 800.

FireWire can provide power up to 45W, compared to USB 2.0's 2.5W. And USB2.0 only supports cable runs up to a maximum of 4.5m (100m for optical FireWire cables).

But USB 2.0 still has a place in the grand scheme of computing things, primarily for less demanding devices that don't require high bandwidth or guaranteed data delivery.

Make the connection

Cables for connecting peripherals are always a consideration. SCSI's short-run, heavy and thick cables were limited and difficult to handle, even though latest developments have improved on the length of the runs.

The FireWire spec allows for up to 4.5m cables, the same as USB, but optical (glass fibre) cables can be used to enable runs up to 100m – ideal for studio use and venue events. This means, just to spell it out, that you could set up computers in one room, with controllers and interfaces in another, entirely isolating any hum, fan noise, disk whirs or other computer noises from the recording environment.

FireWire devices can be daisy-chained, with up to 16 devices in the chain, although it's probably neater to use a hub.

Apple's FireWire 400 connectors use six wires, Sony's iLink, as we've mentioned, uses four, and FireWire 800 uses nine. You can use FireWire 400 and 800 devices on an 800 line, but you'll probably need an adaptor. There are adaptors for 4-to-6 pins and 6-to-9 pins. As ever, these currently come at a premium and typically cost from £20 upwards. The price of technology...

The future

Although FireWire 400 has been the standard for a while, certainly on the Mac, it has the potential to go much faster. IEEE-1394b, implemented in 2002, led to FireWire 800 and lays the groundwork for speeds of 1,600Mbps and then 3,200Mbps as future releases roll out.

We're already seeing the fruits of these developments as Apple's new 17-inch PowerBook G4 sports a FireWire 800 socket as well as a FireWire 400 socket.

The mLAN plan

Another exciting development for musicians is mLAN, a music networking system developed by Yamaha. Essentially, it uses special mLAN chips to transmit MIDI, audio and sync data over a standard FireWire connection.

First generation mLAN was limited to eight audio channels per device, but a second-generation chip overcomes that limitation. In theory, with mLAN equipment you should simply be able to link any kind of music equipment together, from computers and synths to signal processors and mixers, via FireWire without any interfacing problems.

mLAN has been around for a few years, but the higher cost (each device requires an mLAN chip), particularly when compared to MIDI, has meant take-up has been slow and installation has only been seen on a dribble of up-market gear. The latest is Yamaha's 01X Music Production Studio, which will help raise the mLAN profile. But mLAN needs widespread incorporation – much like MIDI in the 80s when a manufacturer didn't dare to release an instrument without those sockets – before it will become universally accepted. But this is very likely to happen…

So the future of music could be mLAN, with FireWire at its core. At the very least, FireWire offers many advantages for both general computer users and musicians, so when you're contemplating a new device, check to see if a FireWire version is available. That could well help to future-proof your system, while offering improved performance at the same time.

Further info

Since Apple was largely responsible for developing FireWire, the Apple site is a good place for more information:

www.firewire.org
www.apple.com/firewire
http://developer.apple.com/firewire
Microsoft's take on IEEE-1394 is at
www.microsoft.com/hwdev/bus/1394/default.asp
And the homepage of the IEEE-1394 organisation is at
www.1394ta.org
For more on mLAN look at these two sites
www.yamahasynth.com/pro/mlan
www.yamaha.co.jp/tech/1394mLAN/english

Tech terms

Isochronous data transfer
This guarantees that data is transferred on time and data packets are received in the correct order. This is used for real-time transmission of audio and video data.

Asynchronous data transfer
This enables the intervals between data transmission to vary according to the available bandwidth. It's not suitable for real-time, critical data transmission, but it's fine for backing-up data to a hard drive, for example.

Enumeration
The process of assigning devices a number. When the computer powers up, it queries all FireWire devices and automatically assigns them an ID number, unlike SCSI where devices must be manually assigned a number beforehand.

FM synthesis

In this increasingly subtractive world, it's sometimes hard to remember there are other synthesis systems just as worthy of our attention. FM synthesis, even with its reputation for being cold, clinical and difficult to program, remains a useful contrast to the sound of analogue subtractive synthesis.

Despite having to get to grips with new terminology, such as operators and algorithms, the basic principals of FM synthesis are reassuringly simple – often using techniques borrowed from subtractive synthesis. Current FM implementations in software (Native Instruments' FM7, for example) are a logical move, solving many of the old problems such as programmability and inferior sound quality. Maybe it's time you gave FM another look...

The beginnings

John Chowning – the Robert Moog of digital synthesis – discovered the principles of FM while experimenting with an early computer music system called MUSIC 5. Realising the potential of what FM had to offer, he tried without success to sell the concept to various American synth manufacturers. In the end, it was Yamaha – a relative outsider to the synth market of the time – that took on the idea and developed FM synthesis into a commercial success. Yamaha produced a number of synths based on Chowning's research (including the GS1, DX1, TX812 and FB01) but it was the six-operator DX7 that went on to be the greatest success of them all, and the machine that defined the sound of FM.

By the late-80s the DX7 and FM synthesis had fallen out of favour. The once-shiny sound of FM seemed outmoded and clinical compared to sample-based synths, such as the Korg M1, that offered more realistic piano and string sounds. As a result, Yamaha gradually phased out FM as its principle system for synthesis, despite the occasional appearance of devices such as the FS1R and DX200 over the years.

It was with the release of Native Instruments' FM7 that FM synthesis finally re-appeared as part of the contemporary studio, offering both a faithful reproduction of the DX7's classic presets and a much-needed overhaul of FM technology that included different waveshapes and filters.

The basics of FM

The simplest example of an FM sound generator would utilise two oscillators – one oscillator modulating the frequency of the other, hence the term Frequency Modulation (FM). In a conventional synthesizer, an LFO (low-frequency oscillator) is used to modulate the pitch, or frequency, of an audio oscillator. The LFO is pitched well below human hearing (1–25Hz) and modulating the audio oscillator creates the effect of vibrato.

But what if we were to increase the pitch or speed of the LFO, right up to or even greater than the speed of the oscillator that it's modulating? Not surprisingly, the effect ceases to sound anything like vibrato – instead, we perceive the result as a change in timbre, with the waveshape taking on a more clanging, bell-like quality. Also, now that we're into the realms of FM, the terminology changes and the real fun starts!

The configuration described here is made up of a 'carrier' and a 'modulator' – the carrier is the audible oscillator, and the modulator is used to modulate the carrier's wave (the modulator is not audible in the final result). To change the quality and intensity of the effect we can change the pitch of the modulator (to create different partials) or change its amplitude (to change the intensity of the modulation and number of harmonics).

Envelopes and filter sweeps

By adding an envelope generator across the output of the modulator oscillator, we can introduce some dynamic timbral movement into the equation. As we've seen, increasing the amplitude of modulator intensifies the amount of additional harmonic material, transforming the sound of a sine wave (the principle waveshape used in FM) to something akin to an unfiltered pulse or sawtooth waveshape.

If a basic A/D (attack/decay) envelope is used to control the amplitude of the modulator, we can create a pseudo filter sweep, with the timbre of the carrier becoming smoother as the note progresses. However, although the analogy of an analogue synth and a sawtooth wave has been used, the results sound very different to a traditional subtractive sweep, but unique and interesting nevertheless.

The DX7 was one of the first commercial synthesizers to feature 'rate/level' envelope generators, which had a significant effect on the range of sounds the DX could produce. Unlike the easier, but more limited, ADSR envelope generators, rate/level envelopes can produce any number of interesting shapes and movements, such as double attacks.

Adding slight feedback to an algorithm (top example) creates additional harmonic material akin to a sawtooth wave. Extreme feedback (bottom example) produces an almost noise-like effect.

A basic FM configuration built from two operators, with a carrier and modulator. The modulator's level defines the harmonic content.

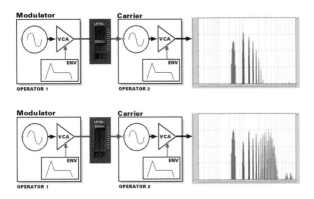

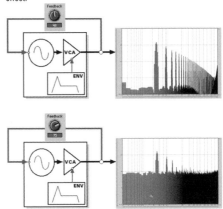

Each step of the envelope has two parameters: the rate the step is taken at, and the final level it reaches, alongside a given break point used to define the sustain. Where an envelope is assigned to a carrier, rather than the modulator example, it can be used to control the overall amplitude characteristics – in the same way that a traditional VCA is controlled by an ADSR envelope.

Call the operator

Using two oscillators configured as carrier and modulator (with associated envelope generators to define the amplitude and timbre), we can begin to create some primitive, but effective, FM sounds and textures. In FM terminology the combination of oscillator, VCA and envelope generator is called an 'operator', which functions as the building blocks of an FM synth.

If we want to go further, we'll need to increase the operators to widen the range of sounds we can produce – ideally, the greater the number of operators, the greater the possibilities. Lower-priced FM synths, such as the DX100, DX27 and FB01, all featured four operators, while professional synths, such as the DX7, offered six. But now we've got six operators what can we do with them?

Algorithms

Linking two or more operators together creates an algorithm. Some operators in this configuration will be working as carriers, others will be acting as modulators – this order and arrangement will therefore have a big effect on the type and range of sounds an algorithm produces. The original DX7 offered 32 preset algorithms that covered most of the conceivable combinations. To create harmonically complex sounds use stacked operators, each modulating the next operator until the final carrier is reached.

The algorithm structure has a big effect on the sound you produce – here are two examples from the original DX7 (and a re-creation on the FM7). Algorithm 1 works best with rich, complex sounds. Algorithm 31 is better suited to simple, additive organ sounds.

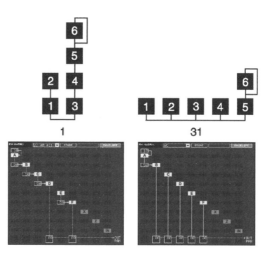

By contrast, using multiple carrier operators (tuned to harmonic intervals) and no modulators, the DX7 can be turned into an additive synthesizer – great for creating organ sounds. Combinations of stacked modulators and additive carriers can also be good for creating hybrid sounds – an amalgamation of bells and strings, for example.

The final, all-important piece of the algorithm puzzle is feedback. Feedback routes an operator back on itself to create an increasingly rich self-modulation. Used subtly it can add distortion or bite to the sound. Whereas at extremes, the density and complexity of the added harmonic material will sound almost like white noise.

Tuning in

When an operator is used as a modulator, the pitch has a significant effect on the type and amount of harmonics that are generated through the process of frequency modulation. Understanding this relationship (between the pitch of the modulator and carrier and the resultant harmonic output) is key to a full understanding of FM synthesis, and an ability to predict the results of modulation. Much of Chowning's research led to a mathematical quantification of this behaviour, although you can still learn a lot through listening to the results you obtain.

Unusually for most synths, the pitch of the various operators is expressed as a ratio of the note played, rather than semitones and cents. In this way, the tuning has a direct correlation to the harmonic series – so 1.000 would be the fundamental, 2.000 would be the second harmonic (an octave higher), 3.000 the third (an octave and a fifth) etc. Tuning the modulator to a fixed ratio results in a harmonically related output (ie. it sounds musical), whereas odd divisions create more clanging, metallic sounds. Raising the pitch places the harmonics further up the harmonic series, producing a sometimes hollow, but also bright, timbre.

What the future holds

With up to six operators per patch – each with its own set of tuning, feedback and envelope control parameters, things can soon get out of hand. Couple this with the DX7's tiny, two-line LCD screen and you can see how the DX7 got such a bad reputation for its programmability. Thankfully, most of these criticisms seem less relevant once you start working with a good software editor and can easily visualise the parameter settings. If you're new to FM sound design, remember that even simple things, such as changing the algorithm or re-tuning the operators, can have a dramatic effect on the sound without having to delve deep into the programming architecture.

Now almost 40 years old, FM synthesis has truly come of age, yet it can still produce contemporary cutting-edge sounds that put many subtractive synths to shame. As a unique sound design tool, its ability to create harmonics, rather than just filter them away, means that FM synthesis is here to stay.

Further info

For more information on Yamaha's much-loved classic DX7, take a look at these four sites:
www.soundofmusic.se/synth/dx7/dx7.htm
www.thedx7.co.ukwww.math.uga.edu/~djb/html/dx7.html
www.synthzone.com/yamaha.htm
To get to grips with the maths behind FM visit:
http://tyala.freeyellow.com/2fmsynth.htm
For a free, non-real-time PC DX7 emulator (the DXulator) visit:
www.tillaart.tk

Tech terms

Additive synthesis

Additive synthesis works by combining a large number of sine wave oscillators to model each harmonic of a given sound. Tonewheel organs (such as the B3) are considered rudimentary examples of additive synthesizers.

Break point

Break points define the points of transition of a rate/level envelope generator (ie. between step 1 and step 2) . The more break points a rate/level envelope generator offers, the better it is.

Partial

Partial is another term used to define a harmonic (ie. frequencies above the fundamental).

White noise

White noise contains an equal mix of all frequencies across the full audio spectrum, and therefore has no discernible pitch. Noise is a useful addition when synthesising flutes or snare drums.

Granular synthesis

Granular synthesis has increasingly become the buzzword of contemporary music production, with a constant stream of artists revealing granular synthesis as the secret weapon in their audio armoury. Despite its origins in the academia of university music departments, granular synthesis is now fully embraced by a generation of musicians wanting to explore more extreme and exciting forms of sound creation. Indeed, artists such as Autechre, Aphex Twin and Richard Devine are more likely to be found dissecting and mangling existing sounds using granular techniques than they are to be hunched over a dusty old modular synthesizer.

Despite its apparent complexity, the principles of granular synthesis are surprisingly straightforward. Unlike most other forms of synthesis, which could be classed as frequency-based (in other words, techniques to modify the frequency components of a given input), granular synthesis works in the time domain, by slicing up and rearranging a sequence of microscopic grains of sounds. Given the level of detail involved (most treatments are synthesised from tiny, 20ms bursts of audio data) the 'sound' of granular is immensely characteristic, often creating harsh, abstract tones alongside complex forms of sound movement. Most interestingly, however, granular synthesis is an opportunity to step inside and utilise the quantum dimension of sound.

The three main parameters of granular synthesis specify the grain size, the distance between grains and an envelope to smooth out any discontinuities.

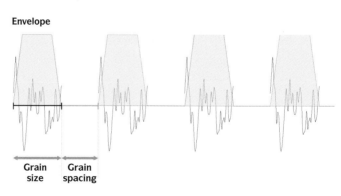

Envelope

Grain size   Grain spacing

From rhythm to pitch

The idea of cutting up sound and rearranging it to build new forms was initially conceived during the musique concrète movement – particularly in the work of Pierre Schaeffer. However, it was the work of composer Karl Stockhausen in the 50s that illustrated the cosmic leap to be made by a more microscopic application of sound editing and synthesis. His proposals centred on understanding how our ears decode pitch, rhythm and timbre over time. A series of short impulses, for example, played about 100ms apart will be perceived as rhythm. If the impulses are bunched closer together – say, 20–30ms – our ears will perceive the impulses as a complete sound at a note of a given pitch. Therefore, the difference between rhythm and pitch is just a small, conceptual dividing line between the repetitive frequency of beats and the repetitive frequency of a waveshape's oscillation.

As an example of this, consider the sound of a super-fast 1/64th drum fill used in drum'n'bass. Technically, the sound is simply repeating at a very fast rate, but our ears don't decode it in that way; instead, we perceive it as a homogeneous sound, with a metallic pitched quality. Change the tempo of the track or the space between the divisions and you'll change qualities of the sound's pitch. Change the choice of drum sound or add a small, velocity

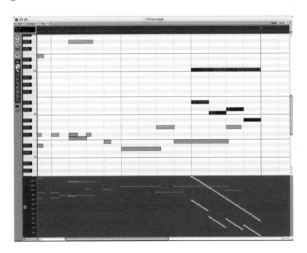

Creating 1/64th fills can create an effect similar to granular synthesis – in other words, creating new sounds from short fragments of audio data.

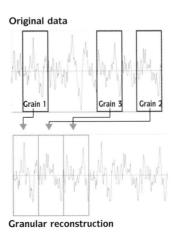

Original data

Grain 1   Grain 3   Grain 2

This example illustrates a typical granular reconstruction, using small 20ms grains of sound, re-sequenced into a new form.

Granular reconstruction

Tech terms

Grain cloud

The grains of granular synthesis can either be arranged sequentially or scattered in a pseudo-random way. The scattered approach to grain distribution is often referred to as a grain cloud.

Zero-crossing point

A perfect edit point between two digital signals can be achieved when the in and out points cross at zero amplitude – in other words, the zero-crossing point.

Cycle ratio

The ratio between the on and off states of a square or pulse waveshape. Changing the cycle ratio has an effect on the harmonic content – anything less than 50% is thinner, but denser in harmonics.

fade-out across the duration of the fill and you'll modify the sound's timbre and amplitude characteristics. Taking the concept even further, you can try switching different drum sounds throughout the duration of the fill, creating timbral movement as the sound progresses.

A grain of truth

The example described above is a crude, but effective form of granular synthesis – in other words, creating new sounds from a series of short acoustic events. To use the correct terminology, the short components that make up a granular sound are referred to as grains, and can be derived from any segment of sound lasting no more than about 35ms in length. Un-looped, the sound would appear as a short click, but if looped or tied into a sequence of grains, we hear it as a complete sound. Usually, the raw material for grains tends to come from short segments of digital audio data, as with even a seemingly insignificant amount of data, the granular synthesist has the potential to create a whole universe of sound.

One easy way to extract and play with sound grains is to use either a sample editor or a sampler's loop functions. By selecting small, single-cycle fragments of the sample, the editor or sampler can be turned into a static form of granular synthesizer. If the position of the loop can either be modulated or shifted, then the granular synthesis can be made to produce a more animated effect. Using this technique can transform any number of source audio files into harmonically rich, grating textures and pads, with each grain offering the potential of radically different timbres.

To soften the results – and offer a greater range of possible outputs – a true granular synth usually provides the ability to envelope each grain, as well as specifying the distances between grains. By enveloping the grains, any discontinuities between the end of one grain and the start of another can be ironed out, creating a true zero-crossing point. Without this feature, a break between two samples could produce clicks between each grain.

The silver lining

Until recently, it was hard to find granular synthesis implemented in commercial products, but now there are plenty of ways to start exploring the principles involved. Of all the current developers, Native Instruments is probably the most keyed in to granular techniques. Absynth 3, for example, includes a granular oscillator as well as conventional oscillators, so a sample can be manipulated with granular principles. The best examples, however, are contained in Reaktor 5, which includes several ensembles based on granular principles. Interestingly, Reaktor is capable of granular processing on both pre-recorded sample data and as a live, real-time effect.

Many sound designers have noticed the link between wavetable synthesis and granular synthesis. Indeed, conceptual parallels can be drawn – and in the case of Reason 3.0's Malström synth, the two techniques of synthesis have fused to create graintable synthesis. In Malström, rather than selecting

Reason 3.0's Malström synth uses graintable synthesis – a combination of wavetable and granular principles. Factory samples are granularised and placed in wavetables.

a waveshape, a 'granularised' sample is called up as a starting point for sound, with the index slider used as the means of stepping through the looped grains.

Stretching time

The techniques of granular synthesis open up a number of new possibilities for sound design. Imagine, for example, grains taken from two alternate samples: the resulting sound would assimilate qualities of both inputs. Granular processing has also become an important facet as far as freeing up the time and pitch qualities of samples is concerned (as exemplified by Kontakt's Time Machine). In this mode, the sample playback comes under the control of a granular engine, so the speed of playback is defined by the rate of movement through the grains.

Sounds new

As more musicians drop conventional instruments and concentrate on sound creation, maybe we should reconsider The Beatles' reign as 'inventors of modern music' in preference to the work of Stockhausen. You only have to look at the success of glitch and stutter edits to realise how interested the ear is in decoding fragments of sound. Once the assumption would have been that granular music would be impossible to listen to, but modern exponents are proving that granular synthesis opens up a new world of musical experiences.

Further info

The ultimate read on the principles of granular synthesis by one of its greatest exponents: *Microsound* by Curtis Roads (ISBN 0-262-68154-4)
For more information on the principles of granular synthesis
visit:www.granularsynthesis.live.com.au/what.html
For some popular granular applications visit:
www.audioease.com/Pages/Free/FreeMain.html
http://meowing.ccm.uc.edu/softmus.htm
www.audiomulch.comwww.crusher-x.de

Harmonics

Ask a guitarist about harmonics and the chances are he'll know a bit about the subject. He'll start banging on about proportions of string length, set into simple motion, which is to a point correct. But what harmonics are goes much deeper than just this. They are, in fact, an intrinsic part of every sound we hear; especially sounds we regard as musical. In this article we'll look at what harmonics are, what causes them, why we'd notice if they weren't there, and why they play an incredibly important part in everything we hear.

In order to understand the theory of harmonics, it's perhaps a good idea to examine how sound works – that is, what actually happens in the physical world when something makes a sound, how we perceive it and how sound is interpreted, stored and replayed by a digital audio device.

What is sound

Sound is essentially a series of compressions and rarefactions (thinning) of air that we call a sound wave. More or less anything in the physical world can cause these waves, but for the purposes of our examples, we should take the example of a loudspeaker.

Imagine a single speaker that's playing a single, simple tone at concert A pitch. For the techies among you, that would be a sine wave at 400Hz. In fact, most synths will have a basic sine wave sound somewhere in their presets, so if you don't know what a sine wave sounds like, select that preset and play an A above middle C and take a listen.

If the speaker is playing a single sine wave sound at 440 hertz, what exactly is it doing? At precisely 440 times a second the speaker cone is mov-

Frequency and its interpretation: The sound waveform on the left can also be interpreted as a description of the movements a speaker cone has to make to reproduce the same sound.

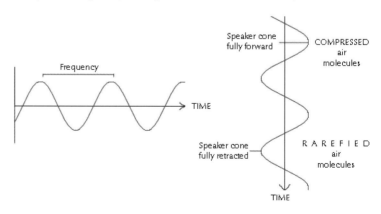

ing smoothly forwards and backwards; as it moves forwards it is compressing the air molecules in front of the speaker cone; as it moves back into the speaker cabinet it is rarefying the air molecules by an equal amount. These compressions and rarefactions of air are moving into the room at high speed – at the speed of sound, in fact.

When these compressions and rarefactions of air molecules hit our eardrums, the membranes in our ears are moved backwards and forwards at the rate of 440 times a second. This produces tiny electronic signals that are fed to the brain, which being a jolly clever organ, translates the electricity into a consciousness of us hearing a simple sine wave tone at concert pitch A.

There is a world of difference between a single sine wave and any other sound source. This is because most sounds that we hear consist of many different frequencies of pitch. In the case of a musical note, we refer to it by its by its fundamental frequency, but we also hear its harmonics (there are also often other frequencies called partials, but more of these later). A sound's timbre is defined by the relative levels of its harmonics to themselves and also to the sound's fundamental frequency.

Good vibrations

Sounds complicated? Not so – here's an example. Let's say we play a fairly low sound at a frequency of around 100Hz. As well as vibrations at the fundamental pitch of 100Hz, there will be harmonics at 200Hz, 300Hz, 400Hz and so forth, up to (and often beyond) the extent of human hearing. These frequencies correspond to fractions of the actual length of a vibrating object – a guitar string, or a column of wind in, say, a flute. The relative strengths of these different patterns of harmonics are what create the comparative differences in timbre or tonal characteristic between various instruments: oboe over bassoon, squealing Strat over eight-string lute. Harmonics (or periodic waveforms) occur at exact multiples of the fundamental frequency, so for a C at 64Hz, harmonics sound at 128Hz, 192Hz, 256Hz (2x64Hz, 3x64Hz, 4x64Hz) and so on up through the harmonic series.

The harmonic series: Harmonics represented in musical notation. An arrow before the note means slightly sharp, a horizontal line means slightly flat.

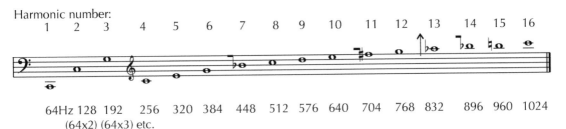

Harmonic number:
1   2   3   4   5   6   7   8   9   10   11   12   13   14   15   16

64Hz 128 192   256   320 384   448   512 576   640   704   768 832   896 960 1024
(64x2) (64x3) etc.

The theory of harmonics explains why we can hear full-on fat bass lines when listening to music through tiny Walkman-style earpieces, or why we can tell Barry White has a deep voice over the phone (and Barry, please stop calling me 'man'). Very small objects – such as Walkman earpieces or the diaphragm of a telephone – simply cannot vibrate at low frequencies; they're too small. However, they can reproduce the higher harmonics of the funda-

Tech terms

Harmonics and partials

The former refers to frequencies that are exact multiples of the fundamental pitch. The latter are frequencies that fall between the harmonics. A pitched instrument produces more harmonics than partials. The situation is reversed with percussive instruments. However, these definitions founder somewhat with instruments and sounds that fall somewhere between: instruments such as struck bells, tubular bells and pitched percussion.

Frequency

Denoted in hertz (Hz) or kilohertz (kHz), it describes the number of oscillations or vibrations per second. We also use the word 'pitch' to describe more or less the same thing. If a speaker moves back and forth 440 times a second, we say that a sound of frequency 440Hz is being created.

mental frequency of lower sounds, and our brain (that clever organ again) can still identify the fundamental pitch because of its pattern of harmonics. This neat trick is called fundamental tracking, or periodicity pitch tracking.

Grey matters

So, when we hear a sound – or rather its fundamental frequency and accompanying harmonics – we assign it a pitch unconsciously, regardless of whether we hear the fundamental pitch. It's difficult to stress quite how difficult this process is; no computer has ever been able to do it with even the simplest combination of sounds. And yet we are hearing, appraising and absorbing sounds constantly, all without a moment's thought.

The number of frequencies we can hear and assimilate is mind blowing. The multitude of sounds from a busy city street may well be largely ignored, unconsciously blanked out by our minds. Concentrate on the sound created by a full classical orchestra, however, and we can distinguish a single instrument's melody and timbre amid the thousands of frequencies present at any one moment!

From a very early age we learn to distinguish timbre. Timbre can be regarded as the 'characteristic' of any individual noise. From when we were babies we were able to distinguish our parents' voices from all others. How? Each voice (and indeed musical tone) has its own unique set of relative volumes of harmonics and fundamental frequency. The human voice is a very complicated example, consisting as it does of many thousands of tones from the vocal chords, affected by movements of the mouth, tongue and lips, and finally shaped by the various hollow and resonating cavities of the human skull.

Take as an easier example, the C below the bass stave given in the musical example above. A double bass playing that note would sound different from an electric bass playing the same. Why? Because the resonating objects that help create the sound are different, there will be a huge discrepancy in the nature of the harmonics that sound at 128Hz, 192Hz, 256Hz and so forth, not only in their volumes, but also in their individual amplitude envelopes.

The next time you apply EQ to your favourite sounds, bear in mind exactly what's going on. By boosting or cutting various frequencies of a sound, you are in fact enhancing or deteriorating the intrinsic tonal quality of the original by cutting or boosting the relative level of the harmonics that make it unique. Try to memorise that phrase – and also the phrase 'periodicity pitch tracking' – for the next time you're hoping to impress a member of the opposite sex.

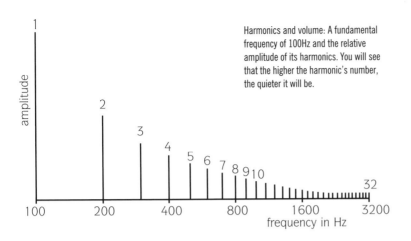

Harmonics and volume: A fundamental frequency of 100Hz and the relative amplitude of its harmonics. You will see that the higher the harmonic's number, the quieter it will be.

Further info about harmonics

There are a number of good places to point your web browser if you'd like more detail on harmonics and sound theory. There's a feature by Scott Lehman that discusses the physics of plucked strings, on the Harmony Central website at
www.harmony-central.com/Guitar/harmonics.html.
You might also want to visit
www.planetoftunes.com/sound
– a good site for features on sound theory, including the nature of harmonics.

More tech terms

Amplitude
A measure of the intensity of the compressions and rarefactions of air caused by a sound source. The more intense the compressions are, the louder the sound.

Timbre
The tonal characteristics of a sound, defined by the relationship between a fundamental frequency and its harmonics and partials.

Microphones

As with many aspects of recording, there's never a 'right' answer when it comes to choosing a microphone. We can, however, greatly simplify our choice by understanding the two main characteristics of a mic: the pickup type and the pickup pattern.

There are two main pickup types (although there are other derivatives that we'll touch on) and three main responses or pickup patterns.

How mics work

Most mics work in essentially the same way; they have within them some light material called a diaphragm, and when sound waves hit the diaphragm it vibrates generating an electric current (the audio signal in electronic format) which is then fed to an amplifier, mixer or recording device. The main difference between microphone types is the diaphragm and the mechanism used to generate the electrical signals.

Dynamic mics

The diaphragm in dynamic mics consists of a thin membrane, usually plastic or metal, attached to a coil of wire that sits inside a magnetic field. The field may be generated either by a magnet inside the coil or by a magnet surrounding it. When sound waves hit the diaphragm, it deflects and moves the coil into and out of the magnetic field, generating electrical impulses. Because of the way they work, these mics are sometimes known as moving-coil mics. The diaphragm and coil are usually quite sturdy (compared to other mic types), which makes the dynamic ideal for live performances. They can stand up to rough handling better than other mics (you can throw them from hand to hand, but don't try bouncing them off the floor!). Their main weakness is the suspension wires that hold the coil and diaphragm in position; these can snap if the mic is handled too roughly.

Dynamic microphone: A wire coil is physically connected to the mic's diaphragm. As sound waves deflect the diaphragm, the coil is also caused to move with respect to the stationary magnet. This movement induces an ouput voltage in the coil that can be amplified.

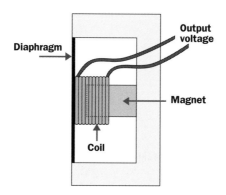

Diaphragm

Output voltage

Magnet

Coil

Dynamic mics are generally good at capturing loud, up-front sounds – another plus for live work – but not so good at capturing quiet sounds and higher frequencies (those over 15kHz). One good thing about dynamic mics is that they're relatively inexpensive. Classic vocals mics include the Shure SM57 and SM58.

Condenser mics

Condenser mics generally have a much lighter diaphragm and work on the principle of capacitance (which is why they are also known as capacitor mics). In a capacitor, an electrical charge is stored between two plates. If the distance between the plates changes, the charge also changes.

The diaphragm is positioned in front of a solid backplate and either of these two components may be electrically charged. When sound waves hit the diaphragm, it moves relative to the backplate, changing the capacitance of the system, thereby generating an electrical signal.

Because the diaphragm is thin, it responds better to high frequencies (up to 20kHz) and quieter sounds, and it produces a more natural-sounding recording. While this would seem to be desirable, some vocals such as rock and punchy stuff can benefit from the inadequacies of a dynamic mic. However, you will often find condenser mics in studios, even for recording vocals, because they're more versatile and responsive.

A condenser mic needs a power supply to power its preamp. This can be a battery inserted into the mic, but more commonly phantom power is used, where available, generally from a mixer.

The downside to condensers is that they're less robust and more expensive than dynamic mics, although recent improvements in microphone technology have improved robustness and reduced prices, too. Popular condensers include the Neumann U47 and the AKG 414.

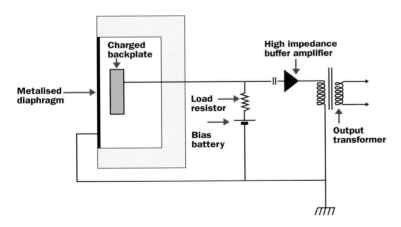

Condenser microphone: These work on the principle of capacitance. As the diaphragm is deflected by sound waves, the distance between it and the backplate alters, thus altering the system's capacitance. The associated electrical circuit is present to convert the change of capacitance into an amplifiable output voltage.

Back-electret mics

The back-electret is a condenser mic, but the backplate features an electret material – which means a material that is permanently charged. This electric charge will eventually wear off, although manufacturers typically claim a life expectancy of 20-25 years. Like condensers, back-electrets also need power.

These mics offer better performance than a dynamic, but are more robust than a condenser. So you get close to condenser performance with greater robustness. Their other major attraction is that they're typically cheaper than condensers.

Other mics

There are several other mic types that deserve a mention. The tube mic is a condenser with valves that offers 'valve warmth', but that must be weighed against the cost, fragility and increased background noise associated with low-level signals.

Ribbon mics are now quite rare, although you may find them in high-end studios. They are a form of dynamic mic that use a ribbon in front of a metal plate. They are extremely sensitive and therefore good for quiet sounds, and they excel at close-mic'ing. However, they're also very fragile and have largely been superseded by condensers except in certain specialist environments.

So-called 'bass' mics are, in fact, merely dynamic mics with larger diaphragms. They are very robust and tend to be used to record sources that generate loud sound, such as the inside of a bass drum, but they have poor high-frequency response.

Pickup patterns

The other aspect of a microphone that you will need to consider when deciding on the best model to use is its response or pickup pattern. Some people think that if you point a mic towards something, that's all it records. Not so; there are three common response patterns. An omni-directional mic can pick up sound equally well from all directions around it. Such a mic is ideal for recording background and ambient sounds, and they also generally lack any proximity effect, so they're commonly used for vocals.

A bi-directional pattern records sounds from in front of and behind the mic (or to the left and right of it, depending on how you view it). Because the response pattern looks a bit like the number '8', such mics are also called 'figure of 8'. Microphones with this pickup pattern might be used to record two instruments simultaneously, or an instrument and some room noise at the same time.

A cardioid response is a heart-shaped pattern, picking up most sound from in front of the mic, a little from the sides and almost none from behind. These are ideal for minimising the pickup of sound that comes from behind the microphone – crowd noise behind a vocal mic at a live performance, for example. Mics with a cardioid pickup pattern tend to minimise such noise rather than eliminate it, and they can be subject to the proximity effect which causes the tone of a speaker's or singer's voice to change as they move closer to or further away from the mic.

There's also a hyper-cardioid design that's a 'tighter' version of the cardioid. It's more directional, has a flatter response and is even less sensitive to sound behind the mic. You might lose warmth, but the benefits in a noisy environment may be worth the trade-off. Live, with monitors on stage, it's a good choice.

Finally, there's a shotgun or directional response mic, which is a more sensitive bi-directional variant. At extremes, these are the sort of mics you see

Omni-directional pickup pattern (left): This pattern of response indicates a microphone that can pick up sound equally well from any direction.

Cardioid pickup pattern (right): Such mics are to some extent directional. They respond better to sound from within the heart-shaped area illustrated above.

being used by 'snoopers' and 'tappers' and people listening in to conversations of individuals in a crowd. FBI stuff. They are not used so much in music.

Putting it all together

Ideally, you will have separate mics for different purposes, such as recording vocals, acoustic guitars, mic'ing drums and so on. In practice, you may not have the luxury or the budget, so here are a few guidelines to help, but do bear in mind that this is where personal preference comes to the fore.

In a studio, the condenser is the most versatile, and a mic with a cardioid response should serve as a good all-rounder. Vocals can benefit from an omni-directional mic, provided there are no sounds in front of the singer. Having said that, some vocalists prefer the response of a dynamic mic because it makes them sound better.

For live use with rock material or vocals that need to be punchy, up-front and in-yer-face, a dynamic mic is the answer. If you need the mic to double in the studio, then consider a back-electret while saving up for separate condenser and dynamic mics.

Recommending a single mic to record a range of acoustic instruments is difficult as different mics suit different techniques. An omni-directional mic can be dangled or placed on a stand in front of an instrument. Condensers would usually be recommended, although dynamic mics are commonly used for mic'ing drum kits. If you can only afford one mic and want a good all-rounder, again a back-electret would be a good choice.

If you get the opportunity to try different mics, you may be surprised at the difference they make to the recording and there's nothing wrong in preferring a dynamic to a condenser for vocals, or a cardioid to an omni if you prefer the sound and can work the proximity effect. That's where art overtakes science in the world of music.

Further info

There's plenty of information about mics on the web, but one of the most useful sources is at:
www.midiman.com/products/tutorials.php
The first item on the page is a 2.49Mb publication in Adobe Acrobat format called *Choosing and Using Microphones*. It tells you everything you need to know about mics.

Tech terms

Phantom power
The supply of power from the ground cable of an XLR connector. The voltage can vary, but it's typically 48 volts. The power can come from the connector to a mixer or a dedicated phantom power box.

Preamp
An amplifier – built-in to some mics – that boosts the signal level, necessary due to the low signal level generated by mics.

Proximity effect
Some mics enhance the low frequencies of a sound source that is close to the diaphragm. This is the proximity effect. Knowledgeable vocalists and speakers can make use of this to good effect, but it can cause problems for the inexperienced.

23 MIDI

MIDI stands for Musical Instrument Digital Interface, and it's basically a communications protocol or set of instructions that enable electronic instruments such as synthesizers, samplers and computers to 'talk' to each other. It was the first widely adopted standard for the transmission of music information and today it's found on virtually every kind of electronic instrument from hardware synths to soundcards.

Where it came from

To understand exactly what MIDI is, what it does and why it was developed, we need to go back to the pre-MIDI days circa. 1981. At that time synthesizers were expensive beasts and sounds were created by twiddling vast arrays of knobs and sliders. Most could only store one sound at a time – no presets here – and they were primarily analogue in nature. That means

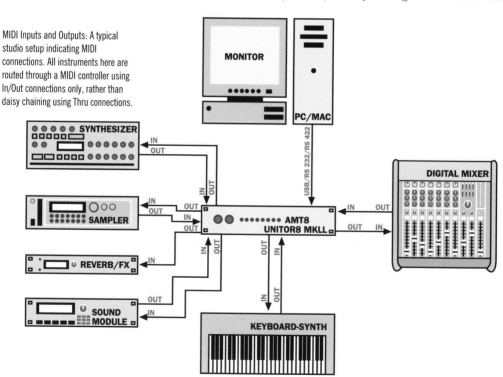

MIDI Inputs and Outputs: A typical studio setup indicating MIDI connections. All instruments here are routed through a MIDI controller using In/Out connections only, rather than daisy chaining using Thru connections.

sounds were produced with analogue circuits such as oscillators, filters, envelope generators (for shaping and controlling volume), low frequency oscillators (LFOs) and so on. Voltages were used to control these modules and shape the sounds. All good techy fare!

In fact, you'll still hear the term 'control voltage' (or CV) used in connection with modern synths (although they generally use digital circuitry to simulate CV control). This technology worked, but because each manufacturer used a different CV system, it was difficult to use one company's synth with another company's sequencer. This effectively tied musicians into using products from just one company.

Fast-forward to 1982 when some developers and companies with a bit of foresight got together to discuss a universal standard for the transmission of musical information. It was originally known as UMI (Universal Musical Interface), but a year later – and after several revisions – it became known as MIDI. By 1986 hardly an electronic instrument appeared without MIDI sockets.

How it works

The main thing to remember about MIDI is that it handles music 'data' or instructions; it doesn't transmit 'sound' in any form. So when you press a key on a MIDI keyboard, a Note On message is generated by the hardware; when you release it, a Note Off message is the result. If these instructions are sent to another synth, the second instrument will play the note exactly as if it were being played on its own keyboard.

Note messages also carry Velocity information with them, which is how hard the key was pressed, and this is normally used to control the volume of the note. However, the actual 'sound' selected on the controlling keyboard is not transmitted. So, for example, if the controller was set to a piano sound and the receiving instrument set to a flute, then the instrument would play a flute sound.

You can change the preset number of the receiving instrument by sending a Program Change message, but this simply selects a different preset, it doesn't send the 'sound' of the controlling instrument to the receiving one. Think about it and you'll realise how impossible sending a 'sound' would be as it would require the second instrument to have exactly the same sound-generation circuitry as the first. This is a common area of confusion for newcomers to music technology and MIDI.

In control

MIDI supports a wide range of musical messages. As well as Note On and Off, there is a group of messages known as Continuous Controller messages. These include Modulation Wheel, Breath Control, Volume, Pan, Expression and more. The total MIDI message set gives you control over most of the nuances of musical performance.

Not all MIDI instruments support all MIDI messages, although the majority of modern ones support most of them. You can discover which MIDI messages an instrument does support by looking at the MIDI Implementation Chart (MIC), which is usually secreted at the back of the instrument's manual.

General MIDI

The standard for MIDI portability, General MIDI (GM) is an agreement between instrument manufacturers about which sounds occupy which preset slots in a GM instrument. For example, Preset 1 is always an acoustic grand piano, 41 is a violin and so on. GM was developed so that music song files in a standard MIDI file format would sound approximately the same when played on any GM-compatible instrument. A GM instrument will still respond to all the usual MIDI messages.

Bits and bytes

For the insatiably curious (and you really don't need to know this if you're not), MIDI messages consist of strings of binary data called bytes. Each byte contains eight bits, each of which can be one of two values: 0 or 1. A single byte, therefore, can represent up to 256 (28=256) values, and sometimes two bytes are used together to give 65,536 (216) values. This is enough to represent most musical instructions in quite fine detail.

Fortunately, most musicians never have to get down and dirty with binary because all sequencers helpfully translate the binary codes into English such as Note On and Off, Pitch Bend, Modulation and so on.

Serial killer

MIDI is a serial protocol, which means that messages are sent one after the other. Most music requires that several events occur at the same time. Playing chords, for example, requires all notes to sound simultaneously. However, via MIDI the notes actually arrive at the receiving instrument sequentially.

So why don't we hear an arpeggio instead of a chord? Mainly because the MIDI protocol is very fast, so although an instrument might technically play an arpeggio, we actually hear it as a chord. However, in pieces with lots of notes or lots of Controller data, the delay is sometimes noticeable. In such cases you may need to thin the data (particularly copious amounts of Controller data). In addition there are MIDI interfaces such as Emagic's AMT8 that incorporate special systems for optimising the transmission of MIDI data to provide more accurate timing.

Ins and Outs of MIDI

There are three types of MIDI connection. Most instruments have all three, but some have just In and Out, and some have just one socket, depending on the type of instrument.

A MIDI Out socket transmits MIDI data generated by the instrument – that's straightforward enough. A MIDI In socket is used to receive data from another source. Again, that's pretty obvious. The MIDI Thru socket passes on a copy of data arriving at the MIDI In socket. This is used to 'daisy chain' instruments together so one keyboard or sequencer can control two or more synths.

It's important to realise that the Thru socket is not a second MIDI Out; it doesn't transmit data generated by the host instrument. At least, usually it doesn't; there are some devices including MIDI Controllers such as the PhatBoy that merge the two data streams, transmitting data that arrives at their In socket along with data they generate themselves through their MIDI Out.

Ins and Outs of MIDI: The M-Audio Ozone is a MIDI keyboard and interface in one. Note the MIDI In and Out connections. As is typical with many devices these days, there is no Thru.

To daisy chain instruments you connect the MIDI Out of the controller keyboard to the MIDI In of the first synth, and then connect that synth's MIDI Thru to the MIDI In of another synth, and so on. In practice, it's far better to use a MIDI Thru box to link instruments.

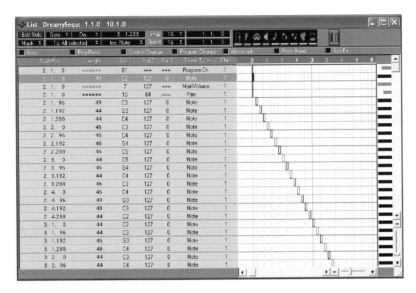

It all makes sense: Modern sequencers automatically translate MIDI messages into plain English such as Program Change, Volume, Pan and Note information, so you don't have to read binary code.

Is MIDI still important?

Most recent music technology developments have been in the field of audio, and many musicians now run complete studios consisting solely of a computer, software and perhaps a controller keyboard. So does MIDI still have a part to play in such systems? The answer is undoubtedly 'yes'. Software instruments such as synths and samplers rely on MIDI data to tell them which notes to play and how to play them.

You might think that if you're only recording audio data you don't need MIDI, but many plug-in audio effects such as EQ, reverb and chorus can be controlled via MIDI messages. MIDI is also commonly used for mixer automation, making it easier to edit mixes rather than create new ones from scratch. And MIDI is also used to synchronise sequencers, either a software and a hardware sequencer, or two software sequencers running on the same computer.

MIDI and modern recording

Virtually every modern recording system uses MIDI in some way or other. If you rely mainly on hardware synths and sound modules or soft synths and samplers, then MIDI is the core of your system. Even if you primarily work with digital audio, you will doubtless have effects that can be more accurately controlled via MIDI. Whichever category you fall into, the more you know about it, the more control and direction you'll have over your music.

Further info

The original MIDI spec was developed by the International MIDI Association (IMA). Although it still seems to be in business, its website has disappeared and the curator of the specs is now MIDI Manufacturers Association (MMA), which has an excellent site at **www.midi.org**. Here you can find more MIDI tech specs and information than you'll ever need or want, a list of MIDI messages and lots of other information and links.

24 Mixers

There was a time when everything was recorded in mono with a single microphone. How simple was that? The only kit you needed was a mic, a mic amp and a recorder. Then, in the 1930s, some bright spark decided that it sounded better if you also laid some close mics on the soloists to bring up the solos in the recording. That meant signals had to be mixed together, and the mixer, as we know it, was born.

History repeating

The earliest mixers had just two purposes: they enabled the engineer to accept multiple input signals and route the outputs to more than one destination; and they offered the engineer the opportunity to adjust the relative levels of these multiple signals with faders to ensure that the output wasn't too loud or too quiet.

Then somebody decided that adjusting the frequency response of the signal might be a good idea and equalisation or 'EQ' was invented – although even in the days of The Beatles, EQ was a switch marked Pop or Classical – in Classical mode the signal went straight through, in Pop mode all frequencies above 5kHz were cut...

In the early 60s, along came 3-track multitrack tape and brought with it the concept of recording some signals while listening back to others. At this point, the mixer started to look a bit like the ones we see today, with sections dedicated to the different functions it has to perform – inputs, groups and monitoring – each with identical controls for all the different ins and outs.

The four mixer sections

So there are two sound sources in a studio: the current live performance, and the stuff playing back from the recorder that has already been laid down. There are also two destinations: the recorder (to record the current performance as an 'overdub' on another track), and the main mix output from where the engineer and the performer listen to a rough approximation of the final result (the 'monitor' mix).

The mixer is, thus, divided up into four areas. The Input section is, of course, where the signals enter. The Monitor section is from where you can listen to the pre-recorded parts. The (sub)Group section is where signals are adjusted for level before they go off to the recorder. Finally, the Master section is where the final mix output controls are lumped together with all the other bits of the mixer that haven't got a home, like control room volume, aux outputs and so on. (Sometimes a section of extra input channels is also included.) Earlier desks generally had these sections split up as in the layout diagram shown right.

| Input channels | Tape monitor returns | Master section | Further output channels (optional) |
| | Sub-group output faders | | |

The levellers

Now let's have a look at the signal diagram for a basic desk shown at the bottom of the page. The lines running along the bottom of the diagram, onto or from which the inputs and outputs feed or take their signal are the 'busses'. The name originates from the metal buss bars that distributed power up and down the length of old factories.

Let's pay a bit more attention to the input stage. As you might already know, the first choice facing you when plugging a signal into a mixer is 'mic' or 'line'? The mixer will only work at its best with a signal that lies between defined level (voltage) limits, so it's the job of the input stage to boost or cut the input signal to match the requirements of the desk. Most 'line-level' signals (synths, outboard, recorders etc.) have outputs that are actually quite close to line and only need a modicum of adjustment to meet with the mixer's approval. These devices will use the 'line' input setting to provide a small amount of trim.

Microphones, on the other hand, have signal outputs a couple of factors of ten below line. Their tiny output signals need to be heavily boosted, and a separate amp section is employed to achieve this high gain. At this stage you will probably also encounter a 'pad', which will shift the gain window of either of these two input stages down by 20dB (to avoid distortion with louder signals), and a phase-reverse switch, which – briefly – makes sure that the mic signal waveforms in multi-mic setups are rising and falling in unison, rather than in opposition, which would cancel each other out. Last, but not least, is the switch for 48-volt microphone phantom power for condenser mics.

Not fade away

We mentioned earlier that performers might need to listen to a different mix to that which the engineer hears, so a separate set of mix faders needs to be provided. These produce a mix totally separate from that made by the engineer, so the source of these signals is before the engineer's faders and unaffected by their movement. This 'auxiliary' mix is routed out from the channel before it passes through the fader, and is called 'pre-fader'.

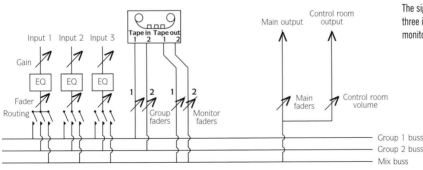

The signal diagram of a simple desk with three inputs, two sends to tape, two tape monitors and a single mono output.

Auxiliaries are fine for 'effects' (that is, processes that take the original signal, mess with it and then add it to the mix from another mixer channel). But what about signal processing that affects the whole signal, such as a gate, or a compressor, or an external EQ? Here we need a mechanism by which we can effectively 'insert' an external processing box into the signal chain by way of an 'insert point'. The insert is provided by a pair of stereo jacks that are specifically wired to break the path when something is plugged in. With nothing plugged in, the signal passes uninterrupted. Some big mixers offer insert points both 'pre-' and 'post-EQ'. It should be noted that on all digital mixers, the analogue insert is before the A/D converters, and thus is pre-EQ.

Pan people

In all the illustrations so far, we've been looking at mono signals for the sake of simplicity. All you need to do to create a stereo mix buss is to have two busses – left and right – and a pan pot to fade the signal between them. A pan pot (or potentiometer) is basically two rotary faders ganged together, but with one fader working backwards. This means that as one gets turned down, the other gets turned up. In the middle position a pan pot will feed equal amounts of signal to both left and right channels.

Do the splits

We've also only looked at split-format mixers so far, and they have one big disadvantage – their size. So what if we incorporated Input Channel 1, Group Out 1 and Monitor 1 all on the same strip of metal? In that case you would have what's known as an 'in-line' mixer, and virtually all recording mixers now follow this format. This makes the mixer around half the width, and thus cheaper. They're also easier to work with, once you've got your head around the fact that all the controls on each channel strip are not actually affecting the same signal path. It also enables auxs and EQs, for example, to be physically switched between the channel strip's input and monitor signal paths, thus making the mixer more flexible and reducing the number of knobs on the desk.

The telephone exchange

A mixer is essentially an overgrown set of switches, so it's not surprising that to offer maximum signal routing flexibility it incorporates a patchbay. This large array of identical jacks is essentially the sockets on the back of every single item of gear in the studio, brought into one place so that routing experimentation can take place without you having to crawl around on the floor.

It also creates a stable grounding environment, regardless of how the gear is actually plugged up. Without it, experimentation is awkward and the consequent unstable earthing of the studio is just inviting interference and noise.

Digital mixers

While we've been talking about analogue mixers here so far, almost all of what has been said applies equally well to digital consoles. Why? Well, because so far all digital consoles have been designed to model the internal architecture of the analogue desks that preceded them. This makes good sense because engineers don't have to learn a new architecture. Indeed, once you've got your head around analogue console architecture, the inner workings of a digital desk will seem an awful lot less complicated. The real power of digital desks, however, is the way in which you can program changes to the internal architecture.

So digital desks ape analogue desks for very good reason, but it can only be a matter of time before someone with no previous analogue desk knowledge gets to design a digital desk the architecture of which will be driven by the designer's own creative experience. The first of this breed may be poorly received, if only because our previous experience of traditional desks will no longer be applicable, but they may well end up being the key to unlocking our creative potential.

Each to their own

Every desk has its own particular characteristics, so here we've only discussed the underlying signal structure that exists in any mixer design, be it analogue, digital or even a software version that resides on your computer. Once you can sit there with your eyes closed and visualise every wire and connection, then the gear will no longer get in the way of your creativity.

Pre-fade: the same mixer input channel with a pre-fader auxiliary (usually on a knob, not a fader) for creating headphone monitor mixes.

Post-fade: it's that mixer again, with a pre- and post-fader auxiliary option for feeding a fader-related signal to reverb and other associated effects.

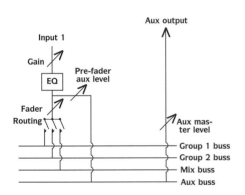

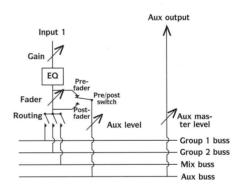

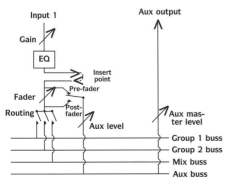

Insert point: this is where you can drop an external processor into the signal path, replacing the original signal with the processed version.

Oscillators

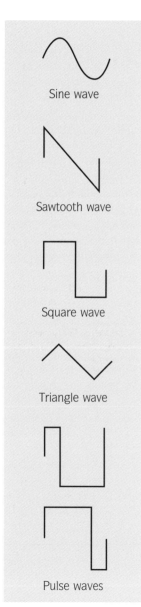

Sine wave

Sawtooth wave

Square wave

Triangle wave

Pulse waves

Virtually every form of synthesis follows three main stages: tone generation, tone shaping and volume shaping. The tone generation part of the process can take several forms, but the most common is the oscillator, which is the main sound source in analogue synthesizers and software emulations.

Oscillators generate sound by, not surprisingly, oscillating. That is, their circuitry changes, or oscillates, between two states very quickly, and just as a vibrating string produces a sound, so the oscillating electronic circuit generates a waveform that can be amplified and used as a sound source.

The output of an oscillator has three parameters: frequency (or pitch), amplitude (or volume) and waveform (or tone). We can see how they relate to a sound by looking at the simplest of all waveforms, a sine wave.

Give me a sine

Oscillators produce repetitive, or cyclical, waveforms that are defined by their frequency in Hertz (Hz). The faster the oscillator vibrates, the more cycles in a given time, and the higher the pitch or frequency of the produced sound will be. The distance from the highest to the lowest points is the waveform's amplitude, and the greater the amplitude, the louder the sound will be. You can see the differences between waveforms of different amplitudes and frequencies in the diagram at the top right of this page.

In control

One of the main features of analogue synthesizers is the way the various modules pass messages to each other; it's all done with voltages. When you press a key on an analogue synth, it sends a specific voltage to the oscillator, which generates a particular pitch. Higher and lower notes produce higher and lower voltages and correspondingly higher and lower notes. Analogue oscillators, therefore, are commonly known as VCOs or Voltage Controlled Oscillators.

Voltage control was used with synth modules such as oscillators, filters, amplifiers and envelope generators. It was such a natural and relatively intuitive method of control that even now many digital synthesizers emulate the VCO routing concept, sometimes quite specifically as with Reason's Control Voltage cabling. Even though digital oscillators don't generate waveforms in the same way as analogue synths, many soft synths adopt analogue synth methods and terminology.

Tone alone

The tone of a waveform is determined by the harmonics it contains. Harmonics are additional frequencies, higher than the fundamental and usually at a lower volume. (See the Ten Minute Master on Harmonics for more on this.)

Harmonics have a natural mathematical relationship to each other; the second harmonic is twice the frequency of the fundamental, the third is three times the fundamental frequency, the sixth harmonic is six times the frequency, and so on.

The harmonics in a waveform determine its shape. We can easily see the amplitude and frequency of a wave by looking at it. However, each waveform has its own harmonic content and its own tone, and it's virtually impossible to know what it will sound like by looking at it. The best approximation we can make is to say that the more complex a waveform is, the more likely it is to have lots of harmonics and to sound richer.

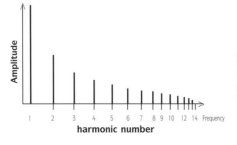

The top two sine waves have the same frequency but different amplitudes, so the sound is at the same pitch but the lower one is quieter. The bottom sine wave has the same amplitude as the top one, but more cycles, so it has the same volume but is of a higher pitch.

Handful of waves

A handful of waveforms are commonly used in synthesis, each with a distinctive wave shape and sound. The simplest is the sine wave, which consists only of a single fundamental frequency. It is often used to synthesise flute and drawbar organ sounds.

A sawtooth waveform contains all harmonics at an amplitude of inverse proportion to their number (with all these mathematical relationships you know something 'natural' is going on). So the second harmonic is half the amplitude of the fundamental, the fifth harmonic is a fifth the amplitude, and so on. Being so rich in harmonics, sawtooth waves are commonly used to synthesise brass, strings and some woodwind sounds.

The square wave contains odd-numbered harmonics only, and in the same proportion as in sawtooth waves. It produces a 'hollow' sound and is used to synthesise clarinets.

Triangle waves contain only

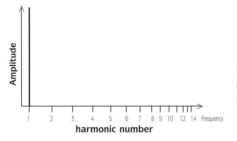

Sine harmonics: A sine wave has only one harmonic and that's the fundamental.

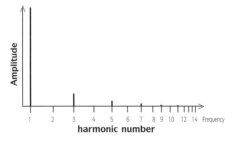

Triangle harmonics: A triangle waveform contains only odd-numbered harmonics of very low amplitudes.

Saw harmonics: A sawtooth waveform contains every harmonic with amplitudes in inverse proportion to their harmonic number.

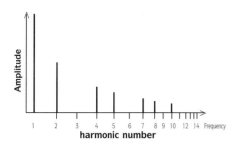

Square harmonics: A square wave contains only odd harmonics with amplitudes in inverse proportion to their harmonic number.

odd harmonics, as with square waves, but at much smaller amplitudes. In fact – prepare yourself for more maths – the relationship is the inverse square of the harmonic number. The third harmonic has an amplitude 1/9th (1/3x3) of the fundamental, the fifth has an amplitude of 1/25th (1/5x5), and so on. Although triangle waves do contain harmonics, they are not very dominant and triangle waves sound very sine-like. Some synthesizers dispense with sine waves in favour of the triangle.

Mark this space

One of the most interesting waveforms is the pulse wave because the wave can be changed to alter its harmonic content. It looks like an offset square wave. Whereas in a square wave the upper and lower sections of a cycle are the same – ie. square – in a pulse wave these can vary. Technically, the upper part is called the 'mark' and the lower part the 'space'. Synth controls for adjusting them are called 'pulse width' or 'mark/space ratio' controls.

The term 'pulse width' is more intuitive, but the mark/space ratio helps us see what harmonics are in the wave. The mark/space ratio isn't actually a ratio between the mark and space widths, but a ratio between the mark and the complete cycle. So, a square wave has a mark/space ratio of 1:2 and the mark is half of the cycle. A ratio of 1:4 means the mark width is 1/4 of the cycle, a ratio of 3:4 means it is 3/4 of the cycle, and so on.

Now, a feature of pulse waves is that harmonics that are multiples of the right-hand ratio number are absent. The square wave with a 1:2 ratio has no even harmonics – harmonics 2, 4, 6, 8, 10 and so on are absent. A mark/space ratio of 1:3 would have no harmonics that are multiples of 3 – harmonics 3, 6, 9, 12 and so on are absent.

As a pulse wave becomes narrower, it becomes thinner and takes on a nasal quality. It is commonly used to synthesise oboe and harpsichord sounds.

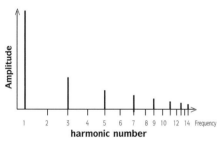

Pulse harmonics: This is a pulse wave with a 1:3 mark/space ratio and it has, therefore, no harmonics that are a multiple of 3.

What's that noise?

The final waveform we'll look at is noise. This is a hissing sound similar to what you hear when a TV signal is lost, or you tune between radio stations. Noise comes in several colourful varieties. The most common is white noise, which contains all audio frequencies in equal proportions. Pink noise is the next most popular; it contains fewer high frequencies, sounds less hissy and has a rushing sound. You can create an approximation of pink noise by running white noise through a low-pass filter (see the Ten Minute Master on EQ.)

Take away

Analogue synths use a process called subtractive synthesis. You start with one of the waveforms just described and run it through a filter to remove some harmonics – hence subtractive synthesis. Most forms of synthesis are subtractive to some degree, as soon as you add a filter to the process you are going to remove something!

One alternative to subtractive synthesis is additive synthesis, which is simply adding waveforms together. If you have enough oscillators – and time and patience – you can try this by adding sine waves together. Create a sawtooth wave, for example, by mixing sine waves at the frequency and proportion of the harmonics as described above.

Home in on the range

As well as generating waveforms, most oscillators have range and tuning controls. Range sets the octave and traditionally this has been calibrated in 'feet', a throwback to the days of organs when the length of an organ pipe determined its pitch. Options will typically be 2', 4', 8', 16' and 32'. Each foot is an octave, and 8' is the octave starting at Middle C. Many modern synths calibrate their oscillators in octaves.

Tuning controls fine-tune an oscillator to a specific pitch. Many oscillators have coarse and fine tuning controls. In the early days of analogue synths, oscillators were notoriously unstable and kept drifting out of tune. They were often switched on hours before a performance to let them stabilise, but the musician would often end up playing with one hand and tuning the beast with another.

Modern instruments are far more stable and digital synths and software should never have tuning problems. However, it's common to run two oscillators together and detune one slightly against the other to thicken the sound.

How low can you go?

We've been talking about oscillators as sound sources, but they can be used as modulators, too. The LFO (Low Frequency Oscillator) is simply an oscillator that oscillates at a low frequency. It could be so low that it takes several seconds or even minutes to complete a cycle.

LFOs are typically used to add vibrato to a sound by applying a sine wave at a frequency of around 5-8Hz to the volume. They can be applied to a filter to produce variations in tone.

Tech terms

Hertz
The unit of 'cycles per second', named after Heinrich Rudolph Hertz (1857-1894). If a sound source vibrates at 100 cycles per second it has a frequency of 100Hz.

Modulator
A synth module the output of which is used to change another.

Further info

On the web take a look at:
http://tyala.freeyellow.com/2ansynth.htm
www.themusicland.co.uk/technology/keen3.htm
www.xgfactory.com/downloads/synthinfo.pdf

Plug-ins

It seems as though every bit of traditional studio hardware is appearing in software form these days. It used to be that you bought a large metal box with lots of plastic knobs to mix your audio. Tape recorders were standard kit, and if you wanted to add effects you bought a bunch of rack-mountable metal boxes with more knobs. And keyboard players bought synthesizers – again, in metal boxes with plastic knobs.

But these days you choose your favourite MIDI and audio software, buy some plug-ins and virtual instruments and away you go.

But it isn't quite as easy as that – VST plug-ins won't work with Pro Tools, MAS plug-ins won't work with Logic, and some formats are specifically designed to work only with particular hardware. Confused? If you are, you're not alone, so let's take a look at all these formats and which ones work with which hardware and software.

What's out there?

Plug-in formats on the Mac include Steinberg's VST and VST Instruments, Mark of the Unicorn's MAS, and Digidesign's TDM, HTDM, Audio Suite and RTAS (Real Time Audio Suite) – for Mac OS9 or OSX. The new kid on the block is Apple's Audio Units (AU) for OSX, which is increasingly being supported by other manufacturers. On the PC, Steinberg's VST and VSTi formats are the most widely supported. The rival DX and DXi formats are also used for audio plug-ins and virtual instruments respectively.

The leading format is VST, for which the largest number of plug-ins is available. Pro Tools TDM plug-ins are the most expensive, but they usually

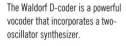

The Waldorf D-coder is a powerful vocoder that incorporates a two-oscillator synthesizer.

offer higher quality than those available for other platforms. Plug-ins running on dedicated DSP cards generally offer higher quality than those running 'native' on the computer's CPU; even when comparing the same plug-in from the same manufacturer.

Third-party support for the MAS format is highly organised, giving MOTU something of an edge over other plug-in manufacturers; and the Mac platform is generally ahead of the PC when it comes to plug-ins, although the gap is closing fast.

What works with what?

On the Mac, Cubase SX/SL and Nuendo make ideal hosts for VST and VSTi formats. However, there can be problems with some versions of Logic running VST plug-ins under OS9, while OSX versions of Logic don't support VST. Instead, Logic uses its own plug-in format, which isn't supported by anyone else. Nevertheless, OSX versions of Logic also support Apple's AU format, which is widely supported by third parties.

Digital Performer 4 supports both MAS and AU formats and MOTU has encouraged many other developers to produce plug-ins in the MAS format. Digital Performer 4.1 and Logic Platinum can also support TDM plug-ins if you have TDM hardware; Sonar, Cubase SX and Nuendo cannot. Most Mac OSX applications now support Apple's AU format – or will do very soon – and this is fast becoming a rival for the VST format.

Steinberg's VST and VSTi are the leading formats on the PC, although support for the DX and DXi formats is increasing. Most popular packages – including Sonic Foundry's Acid, Cakewalk's Fruityloops, Adobe Audition (the application formerly known as Cool Edit Pro), SEK'D Samplitude and Ableton Live – support one or both of these. Cakewalk Sonar and Sonic Foundry's Vegas and Sound Forge all support the DX formats, while Cubase SX/SL and Nuendo, naturally, support VST. WaveLab supports both formats.

Just as the plug-in manufacturers are all rushing to make their plug-ins available in all formats on the Mac, the same trend can be seen on the PC. As far as features are concerned, whether you look at the user interface or the resulting sound quality, there is little or nothing to choose between 'native' Mac or PC versions of most plug-ins. The crucial issue is whether the plug-in you want to use is available for your host software or not. If not, you may want to consider changing your host software – or even changing computer platform! Some recording musicians have even ended up buying a PC just to run GigaSampler, for example, or a Mac just to run Altiverb.

Pro Tools plug-ins

Pro Tools TDM systems, including the HD, MIX and DSP Farm cards, use DSP chips on these cards to process audio using TDM plug-ins. Pro Tools TDM systems can also use Audio Suite, RTAS and HTDM plug-ins that run on the host computer's CPU. Pro Tools LE systems, on the other hand, can use only Audio Suite and RTAS plug-ins.

The way Audio Suite plug-ins work is that you select an audio region, apply the plug-in, preview and adjust the settings, then process the region to produce a new audio file to replace the original region. The advantage is that once you have carried out this operation, the CPU is left free for other tasks. The disadvantage is that it isn't a real-time process.

All TDM plug-ins work in real time – all you have to do is insert these into Pro Tools mixer channels to provide immediate effects as you do with RTAS and HTDM plug-ins. The difference is that with HTDM and RTAS, all the processing is done using the host CPU instead of using DSP chips on the TDM hardware.

DSP cards

The more complex plug-ins seriously occupy the attention of your computer's CPU, so a dual-processor computer running at the fastest clock speeds is a good idea. An alternative is to use dedicated DSP for your plug-ins.

TC Electronic and Universal Audio have both developed PCI cards containing processors dedicated to running plug-ins. These use specially designed plug-ins that run only on these cards – they won't run your normal plug-ins. But you can install and use both UA and TC cards simultaneously, and you can use multiple cards from both manufacturers.

The Universal Audio UAD-1 Powered Plug-Ins system comes with VST and MAS plug-ins that provide reverb, guitar effects and comprehensive channel-strip effects. The UAD-1 also includes plug-in versions of the highly regarded Universal Audio 1176LN and Teletronix LA-2A vintage compressors and the Pultec EQP-1A vintage EQ. The UAD-1 supports DirectX and the various Windows operating systems from Windows 98SE to Windows XP, but as yet doesn't support Mac OSX.

TC Electronic's PowerCore works with any VST-, MAS- or AU-compatible audio application. PowerCore enables you to run at 24-bit/96kHz and use multiple reverbs, compressors and synthesizers, all without maxing out your CPU. The PCI card has been available for some time, but the big news is TC's PowerCore FireWire. This offers almost twice the power of the PCI-card version and works with laptops!

On the PC, PowerCore works with any VST-compatible application, but runs only under Windows 2000 or XP. PowerCore systems come with a great selection of plug-ins including reverbs, modulation effects, EQ, voice channel strip, vintage compressor and the TC 01 Virtual Synthesizer. PowerCore's advantage is that it supports an increasing number of third-party plug-ins from Waldorf, Sony Oxford, TC-Helicon, DSound and others.

Creamware also offers a range of hardware with plug-in soft synths and effects, and Korg offers the Oasys PCI card with a tremendous range of synthesizer and effects plug-ins. The Creamware and Korg cards have audio I/Os and other features that make them more than DSP cards on which to run plug-ins, but they can be used (like the UAD-1 and PowerCore) in this role if you already have I/O hardware.

Other matters...

If you're upgrading to Mac OSX from OS9, you'll need software upgrades for all your plug-ins because OS9 plug-ins don't work under OSX. On the PC it's a little easier – some plug-ins designed for older Windows operating systems will work with XP. However, others won't, so don't make any assumptions. Similarly, some more recent TDM plug-ins will work only on HD systems. Again, if in doubt, check the Digidesign website.

As I said earlier, VST is the most common format. So what if you want to use a particular VST plug-in with software that doesn't support VST? Well, there are several so-called 'VST wrappers' available that enable you to get around this problem. On the Mac, the Audio Ease VST Wrapper (www.audioease.com) enables you to use VST plug-ins with Digital Performer. Cycling '74's Pluggo and Pluggosynth VST plug-in wrappers (www.cycling74.com) come in a package with around 100 plug-in effects and synthesizers. The Fxpansion VST-to-AU Adaptor for Mac OSX (www.fxpansion.com) actually creates AU plug-ins from your VST plug-ins.

On the PC, the Cakewalk VST Adaptor (www.cakewalk.com), formerly available from Fxpansion, converts VST-format plug-ins to DX and DXi formats. DirectiXer (pronounced 'direct-eye-zer'), another VST adaptor for DirectX host applications, can be found at www.tonewise.com/DirectiXer.

To conclude

This area is something of a minefield at the moment, especially if you're upgrading from older operating systems or Pro Tools hardware, but things are getting better – and will continue to do so. Compatibility is still an issue, but you can now get the majority of plug-ins to work with most systems.

Further info

Books

A Professional Guide To Audio Plug-ins And Virtual Instruments. Mike Collins, Focal Press, 2003.
Software Synthesizers: The Definitive Guide To Virtual Musical Instruments. Jim Aikin, Backbeat Books, 2003
Emagic Logic Virtual Instruments: A User's Guide. Stephen Bennett, PC Publishing, 2003. (How To Set Up And Use Logic Audio's Virtual Instruments)
Cakewalk Sonar: Plug-ins And PC Music Recording, Arrangement And Mixing. Roman Petelin and Yury Petelin, Music Sales, 2002.

Websites

Kelly's Music and Computers store buyer's guide for plug-ins
www.kellysmusic.ca/plugins.asp.
Arbiter (UK Distributor for Steinberg, Native Instruments, Akai Professional, Apogee, Arturia, Celemony, Echo, Evolution and Kurzweil)
www.arbitergroup.com
Unity Audio (UK Distributor for Arboretum, Antares, Bitheadz, Kind Of Loud, GRM Tools, McDSP, Wave Mechanics, Audio Ease, Gallery, U & I)
www.unityaudio.co.uk
Universal Audio
www.uaudio.com
TC Electronic
www.tcelectronic.com
Creamware
www.creamware.com

Tech terms

AU
Apple's new Audio Units format

CPU
Central Processing Unit

DSP
Digital Signal Processing

DX
DirectX

DXi
DX Instrument

HTDM
Host TDM

MAS
MOTU Audio System

RTAS
Real Time Audio Suite

TDM
Time Division Multiplexing. Used as a label to distinguish Digidesign's high-end audio cards from their lower-priced products that do not have onboard DSP.

VST
Virtual Studio Technology

VSTi
VST Instrument plug-in format

Reverb

Reverb and echo were arguably the first audio effects man ever discovered, as he grunted in his cave and shouted across a canyon. And the acoustic enhancement of singing and playing instruments in large rooms was well known to the architects who designed theatres, auditoriums and cathedrals. Indeed, the only way for early recording engineers to create reverb was to record in a large room known as a 'live room', but this was costly and inflexible. The earliest artificial reverb devices were large springs and plates, but affordable digital reverb units and delay lines began to appear in the 1980s, followed by software reverb effects in the last few years.

Samplitude's sophisticated Room Simulator uses 'impulse responses' to create realistic reverb effects.

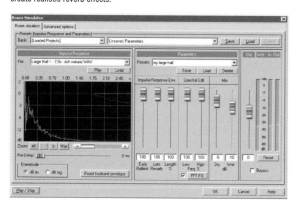

Reverb is a very complex effect that's created by sound bouncing around the environment. If you clap your hands in a large room, for example, not only does the sound reflect from the four walls, floor and ceiling, but those reflections will also bounce around the room like a lot of manic rubber balls. The result is a vast number of echoes that we perceive as a continuation of the original sound.

Reverb occurs in virtually all natural environments, although small rooms, rooms with furnishings and absorbent surfaces, and large fields may seem to be lacking reverb because the sound is quickly absorbed or there are no surfaces for the sound to bounce off. Our ears use the reflections to form an acoustic image of the environment, so by changing the characteristics of the reverb we apply to a sound, we can make listeners think a singer is singing in the bathroom, a concert hall or the Grand Canyon.

In control

Reverb units have become increasingly sophisticated and some offer control over all the parameters that make up the reverb effect. Here's a quick rundown of the major players:

- *Pre-delay* This is the time it takes for reverb to 'kick in', and it contributes to our perception of the size of the environment. A longer pre-delay indicates a larger space.

- *Reverb/decay time* How long it takes the reverb to die away. The longer the reverb time, the larger the environment will appear.
- *Mix* This sets the balance between the wet and dry signals.
- *Early reflections* These are the first echoes or reflections you hear. They're the strongest and the ones that come back at you from the closest surfaces. After these, what you hear are the reflections of the reflections. They also contribute to our perception of the size of the environment.
- *Density/width* This is the time between the early reflections and the rest of the reverb. The shorter the time, the more dense the reverb appears to be.
- *Diffusion* This is how spread out (or diffuse) the reflections are. With low values the reflections are further apart and you may be able to hear them as discrete echoes. With higher values, the reflections are closer together and sound more like reverb.
- *Damping/frequency attenuation* As reflections bounce around the environment, the surfaces absorb various frequencies. These vary according to the surface and how reflective it is. The highest frequencies are inevitably the first to go, but the more reflective a surface is, the longer it takes the higher frequencies to die away, so this gives us another clue about the environment. The longer it takes the higher frequencies to die away, the more 'life' the environment seems to have.

Adjusting all these parameters to produce a realistic reverb can be quite challenging and, of course, you can produce some decidedly unrealistic effects by playing fast and loose with the parameters. If you want realistic effects, it's a good idea to start with the presets and tweak the settings, rather than trying to create an effect from scratch.

Environment simulators

Given the complexity of reverb, several developers have produced more user-friendly effects along the lines of room simulators. They may include parameters such as room size, room shape, liveliness (the high frequency absorption parameter), and room characteristics. Cakewalk's Audio FX3 goes one stage further by enabling you to design your own room, select and position the microphones and place the performers within it.

Some reverbs, such as Sonic Foundry's Acoustic Mirror and the room simulator in Samplitude, use the 'impulse response' of an environment. This is the acoustic response an environment produces in response to an impulse such as a percussive sound. This can be applied to audio tracks exactly like a normal reverb effect. There are dozens of impulse responses for Acoustic Mirror covering environments such as theatres, classrooms, halls, bridges, stairwells and tunnels – and the intrepid experimenter can even create their own impulse responses.

Sonic Foundry's Acoustic Mirror uses 'impulse responses' from natural environments to create authentic natural reverb effects.

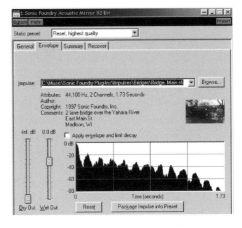

Tech terms

Wet and dry

A dry signal is the original, unprocessed signal. A wet signal is one that has been processed.

Anechoic

Literally 'without echo'. An anechoic chamber is a room designed to absorb all sound reflections and used to test audio equipment.

RT60

The quoted unit of reverb time, which is technically the time it takes for a sound to decrease in amplitude by 60dB.

Ping pong delay

A combination of delay and panning where alternate echoes are panned to opposite sides of the stereo image.

Sing something distant

Because reverberation gives us our perception of the environment a sound is in, we can use it to help create 'artificial spaces' for vocals and instruments. A lot of reverb will give the impression that a vocalist is singing in a cathedral, while very little reverb will make it more up-front and in-yer-face. A natural reverb with average damping may be ideal for a ballad, but you may prefer a livelier sound with less damping for a rock song.

Reverb can also be used to good effect on instrument tracks, to take the dryness out of a synth sound, for example. It is also very popular with drums and a common ploy is to apply reverb to just the snare drum to create a rock drum feel.

The secret of using reverb is not to use too much, yet modern reverb effects seem to positively encourage over-the-top application. It's so easy to 'improve' a sound by cranking up the reverb level, but in a mix it will sound muddy and indistinct, so start with small amounts and add more if required.

Delay and echo cho ho o...

Reverb and echo (or delay) are closely linked as both involve repeats of the original sound. However, whereas with reverb the repeats are so close together that they sound like a continuation of the original sound, with echo the repeats are far enough apart to be individually distinguishable. The words 'delay' and 'echo' are often used interchangeably; technically, a 'delay' could be a delay of any length, whereas you'd expect to hear an 'echo' as an individual sound. Something to be aware of, but not to get hung up on. Many effects even blur the distinction, being able to create so many short delays that the result sounds like reverb.

The first echo units were tape-based and created simply by running a tape loop through first a recording head, and then several playback heads. Famous units include the Watkins Copycat and Roland's Space Echo, both of which were much used by cabaret vocalists. The lure of the tape-based echo unit is such that Steinberg released a tape echo simulation plug-in called Karlette.

Modern delay units are, of course, digital, and with the power and flexibility of software comes increased possibilities for creating new effects. Let's look at the standard controls first:

- *Delay time* This is simply the time between the delays or echoes. There may or may not be a lower limit. Very low values will produce an effect more like reverb than echo.
- *Feedback* This controls the amount of delayed signal that is fed back into the delay loop. With no feedback there will only be one echo. As you turn it up the number of echoes increases and with some effects extreme settings will cause the unit to feed back on itself and go into oscillation.
- *Decay* Not all effects have this, but where they do, this parameter determines how quickly the echoes die away.
- *Mix/Balance* This governs the mix between the original sound and the processed sound.

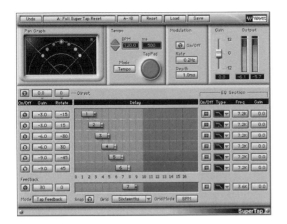

(Left) Waves' SuperTap is a six-voice, multi-tap delay plug-in, useful for creating rhythmic repeats and doubling

(Right) Karlette is Steinberg's software answer to once-popular (and still popular with some) tape-based echo units.

Natural echoes repeat at regular intervals, decrease in volume as they die away and, as with all sounds that bounce off surfaces, the higher frequencies die away first. So to create a natural-sounding echo, you know what you need to do...

Tippety tap

Although natural echoes have regular repeats and die away in a uniform manner, there's no reason why a processed delay should work in the same way. The multi-tap delay unit, therefore, offers several echoes, or taps, and gives the user control over each tap. So, for example, you may be able to specify separate delay times, feedback levels and volume settings for each echo.

Delay and echo are more commonly used with instrument tracks than vocals, but although the modern preference is generally to use reverb on vocals, try echo for a different – and slightly retro – effect.

Sync and pan

One interesting feature of most modern plug-in delay effects is their ability to synchronise the echoes to the tempo of the host sequencer. This opens up a range of rhythmic possibilities that would be either very difficult or impossible to create outside of software.

Some delay units have a pan control that enables you to pan the echoes to different parts of the stereo image. This can create some very interesting and striking effects and, again, would be difficult to do outside of software.

Reverb and echo are essential effects for the modern studio, but – as with all effects – they need to be used with care, and not simply to try to 'beef up' an otherwise average recording.

Further info

www.hairthieves.com/tip/eff/rev.htm
http://audacity.sourceforge.net/docs/effects_reverb.html
http://hyperphysics.phy-astr.gsu.edu/hbase/acoustic/reverb.html
www.sfu.ca/sonic-studio/handbook/Reverberation.html

Samplers

If you're old enough to cast your mind back to 1979 and the early 80s, you may recall that the instrument of desire at that time was the sampler. The Fairlight and the Digital Synclavier, costing more than most of us expected to make in a lifetime, made us drool as they demonstrated the power of sampling technology.

Throughout the 80s samplers became more affordable (although many still cost a year's wages) and then, as the 90s progressed and finally turned into the new century, software samplers began to appear, offering more power and versatility than their hardware forefathers and at much lower prices.

But whether a sampler is hardware- or software-based, they all have a common set of functions and features for arranging and manipulating the raw sample material.

Rates for the job

The first step is to record or sample some material. For a detailed discussion of digital sampling see the Ten Minute Master on Digital Audio (page 48), but briefly, there are two main sampling considerations: sample rate and sample resolution. The sample rate is how many times the source material is read, or sampled, per second – the higher the rate, the more accurate the sample. Audio CDs use a sample rate of 44.1kHz. Many samplers offer rates up to 96kHz, and some even go as high as 192kHz.

The sample resolution is the scale of measurement used to store the sample readings. It's measured in bits and early samplers had a resolution of 8 or 12 bits. You can calculate the resolution by raising 2 to the power of the number of bits. So, an 8-bit system has a resolution of 256 (2^8), and a 12-bit system's resolution is 4,096 (2^{12}). So each sample in an 8-bit system, for example, must take a value from 0 to 255. In terms of reproducing the vast dynamic range of natural sounds, a resolution of 256 isn't going to be terribly accurate. 4,096 is better, but the 65,536 values of 16-bit is better still, and this is the resolution used by CDs. Many samplers now offer 24-bit resolution, which comes even closer to capturing every nuance of natural sound.

So why not simply record at the highest possible

Steinberg's HALion has a Waveloop page where you can set the start and end points of the sample to create loops (there are crossfades to help with this).

sample rate and resolution? One day we will, but the higher the rate and resolution, the more processing power and storage space is required, so at the moment we have to balance what we would like against what we have and what we can afford.

Sample this

Not everyone has access to a symphony orchestra, exotic percussion or the Vienna Boy's Choir, but sample producers do. And through their work we have access to literally thousands of pre-recorded samples. Unfortunately, there's no standard format for samples, so they come in several guises. Most sample producers tend to opt for .WAV (for the PC) and .AIFF (for the Mac) formats, and these are as close to a standard as we have at the moment.

Most of the other formats were developed for specific samplers and it's up to you to decide how important it is for your sampler to be able to read them. In the heyday of the hardware sampler, the Akai sample format was de rigueur. The Sound Designer II (SDII) format used by Digidesign software is still popular on the Mac, and many collections were created for the SampleCell sampler (originally designed for the Mac, but later ported to the PC). Creative Lab's SoundFont (.sf2) format is popular with hundreds of thousands of SoundBlaster soundcard users and is also commonly supported by samplers.

Storage

Early samplers stored their samples in RAM – as indeed do many software samplers. This obviously limits the number and size of the samples you can store and play at any one time. However, increases in computer power have helped enterprising companies to develop software samplers – such as the Nemesys' GigaSampler and Steinberg's HALion – that can read samples directly from hard disk. So, at last, size is not an obstacle.

Going loopy

The memory limitations of early samplers meant you could not store samples of any great length and, therefore, you could not hold a note for very long. The solution to this problem was the loop. You'd find a central portion of the sample and simply repeat it for as long as the key was held down, then jump to the end of the sample when the key was released. Finding good loop points was an art, and a difficult one at that. The problem has been alleviated somewhat by the inclusion of more RAM in samplers and computers, cheaper RAM prices, the ability to store samples on hard disk, and by better looping facilities in the form of audio editors and dedicated loop-finding software.

Root of the problem

The first stage in preparing a sample for playback is to assign it to a root note. This does not necessarily have to be the pitch at which it plays. This is obvious in the case of drums, for example, but it's also useful when creating layers and key splits, as it means that you can play the same pitch from two or more sections of a keyboard.

To play a sample in a realistic manner you need to play a range of pitch-

Tech terms

ADC
Analogue-to-digital converter – the gizmo that samples audio and converts it into digital data.

DAC
Digital-to-analogue converter.

Bit
Short for Binary digIT, a number that can have only one of two values – 0 or 1 – and which is used by computers at their lowest level of operation.

Pitch shifting
Changing the pitch of a sample without changing its duration.

Timbre
Describes the character of a sound.

Key mapping
A general term for the assignment of samples to keys. It covers key splitting, layering and multisampling.

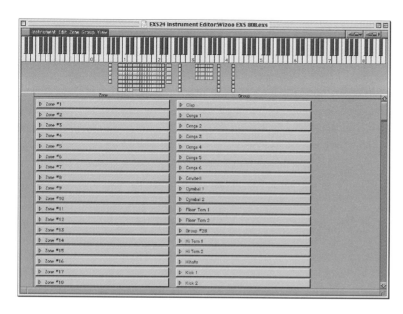

es at different volumes. The simplest way to do this is to assign a single sample to a root note and then play it back faster or slower to produce other pitches. However, this makes the note shorter or longer than the original sample, and the attack phase will therefore be shorter or longer, too. This can be acceptable for pitches three or four semitones away from the root, for example, but you don't have to transpose a sample far from its original pitch before it starts to sound unnatural.

In the Instrument Editor page of Logic's EXS24 sampler you can assign a range of samples to each key, ideal for creating drum sets.

Multi-samples

The way around this is to use more than one sample, a process known as 'multi-sampling'. In an ideal world, each note would have its own sample but, as you can imagine, the sampling process would require considerable effort, and the sampler would need a lot of resources to store and play those samples. But that has not prevented several companies producing gargantuan sample sets such as Steinberg's The Grand, which includes 1.3GB of samples! However, depending on the instrument, it's usually possible to achieve realistic results using a different sample for every three or four notes.

Velocity switching

But simply having a different sample for each note is not always realistic enough. With most acoustic instruments, the timbre of a note also changes with its volume. Louder notes tend to have more high harmonics and often a faster attack time. So we could go another mile and sample each note at several volume levels.

Steinberg's The Grand contains over 1.3GB of piano samples and the control panel enables you to adjust the velocity curve and sound characteristics.

On playback, the MIDI velocity determines which sample is played. This process is known as velocity switching and is set up by selecting velocity points so notes with a velocity below, say, 80, will trigger one particular sample and notes, while velocities of 80 or above will trigger another. This feature works particularly well with drums because their tone changes quite noticeably the harder they are hit.

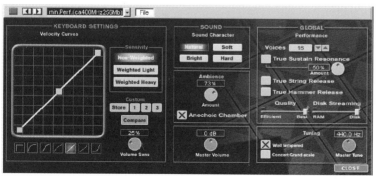

You can do plenty of wild and wacky things with velocity

control such as assigning totally different samples to each velocity value. Try it with drum samples, so that each time you press a key with a different pressure you'll get a different drum sound.

Velocity crossfading

Velocity crossfading uses a feature found in many samplers called 'reverse sensitivity' (or 'reverse velocity'), which reverses the way in which velocity control normally works – so the softer you play, the louder the output is. You set up a string sample, for example, with reverse sensitivity and combine it with a normal piano sample. When you play with average pressure, you'll hear both the piano and the strings. When you play harder you'll hear mainly piano; and when you play more softly you'll hear mainly strings.

Layering and stacking

Layering or stacking is simply assigning different samples to the same key to create mega-combination sounds. Of course, you can combine this with velocity tricks, too.

Key splitting and zones

Samplers have many features to help you set up and organise samples. One is the creation of zones; sometimes also know as 'key splitting'. It involves dividing the keyboard into several sections – say into octaves – and assigning a different set of samples to each zone. This is useful in performance as it enables you to play several sounds from one keyboard, but it's not such an essential feature if samples are being triggered on a computer via MIDI. However, many samplers use the zone concept to help with the organisation of layers and setting velocity levels.

As well as splitting the key range into discrete zones, many samplers enable you to overlap the zones. You could split a keyboard into three sections: the lower playing strings, the upper playing piano and the middle section playing both piano and strings.

Extras

Once upon a time, if you had all of the above features in your sampler you'd be a very happy bunny. Nowadays, most samplers have many extras such as built-in filters and effects, LFOs and envelopes. In fact, many have all the features of a synthesizer, except that samples are used instead of oscillators.

The main strength of a sampler remains its ability to reproduce acoustic instruments and natural sounds, and the flexibility of its programming makes it a valuable instrument in the studio.

Further info

www.baconmusic.co.uk/tutorials/story.asp?contentID=325
www.hitsquad.com/smm/cat/SOFTWARE_SAMPLERS
www.zicweb.com/scripts/get.php?i=15&lg=us
http://machines.hyperreal.org/winky/0033.html?Winky
http://dir.yahoo.com/Entertainment/Music/Recording/Sampling

Sequencers

Ask a number of music professionals to name their favourite sequencer and you're likely to receive completely different answers. Performers might answer Cubase, Logic or Sonar, because those products provide an all-in-one composition, recording and production solution. A music teacher might point you to Band-in-a-Box, because it generates automatic play-along accompaniment for their students. Recording engineers and producers are likely tell you that Pro Tools is the 'guv'nor' because of its high-end audio-editing capabilities. The word 'sequencer', depending on the musical context, can mean very different things to different people.

Wall of sound

To Raymond Scott, the American film composer who's generally acknowledged to have invented the first sequencer as far back as 1953, a sequencer was the giant electromechanical device residing in his laboratory. He referred to it as his Wall Of Sound. According to his friend Bob Moog, the inventor of the Moog synthesizer, it comprised countless racks stacked high with relays, motors, steppers and electronic circuits.

However, despite a great deal of interest and a visit from the bosses of Motown Records, the Wall Of Sound never saw the light of day. You see, Scott wasn't really interested in making money from his invention; he was already a wealthy man. Despite the fact that he was a prolific composer himself, his real goal in life was to perfect an automatic composition machine.

The first commercial sequencers were analogue devices consisting of modules that could be set to particular voltages. When triggered sequentially, these voltages were interpreted by an external synthesizer as a sequence of notes. Such repetitive action was clearly more suited to digital technology and before long these analogue machines were replaced by computers. They're now very hard to find, but Algorithmic Arts has developed software emulations of these beasts – SoftStep and BankStep – which output MIDI data instead of control voltages (CV). If you're a Windows user, you can download demos from the company's website.

A step ahead

For electro composers in the 70s, computerised step sequencers were an absolute boon and ideally suited to the robotic style of music associated with groups such as Kraftwerk. Composers simply typed a sequence, step by step, into machines like the MC-4. The 16 notes of the chromatic scale would be represented by the numbers 12 to 27 and a bar of 4/4 was allocated a number of steps. For example, if a bar had been defined as 192 steps, a half-note (minim) would be entered with a value of 96.

The software equivalent of step entry survives today and can be found in both Logic and Cubase. To try it out in Cubase SX, open a MIDI editor and press the Step Entry icon. Now specify note spacing and length, using the Quantize and Length menus and enter the notes with your MIDI keyboard. In Logic, you can use the Keyboard window. Cubase's Drum editor also provides step entry, as does Logic's Hyper editor.

The Oxford Dictionary defines a sequence as 'the following of one thing after another; a set of things belonging next to each other in a particular order'. To a songwriter, that 'set of things' could be interpreted as an intro, verse, chorus and bridge. Until the 80s, pop music was composed using traditional acoustic instruments and song construction (because that's what composing is – beyond the initial bursts of inspiration, of course) was a mental process. But the advent of the Atari computer and pattern-based software such as Steinberg's Pro 24 and C-Lab's Notator changed all that.

Crazy patterns

Using pattern-based sequencers, musicians could compose complete songs and easily restructure their material sequentially. For example, the centre-piece of the Arrange page in C-Lab's Notator was displayed as a single pattern. Within each pattern were 16 tracks. Musicians would simply record verses and choruses into patterns and assemble them in whatever order they liked in the 'pattern list'. The finished songs, although rather conventional in structure, often had a robotic feel to them. In the mid 80s, this method of writing gave birth to a whole new style of music known as synth pop – think Depeche Mode and Pet Shop Boys.

Steinberg abandoned pattern-based sequencing when Pro 24 was reborn as Cubase. Notator, which eventually became Logic, soon followed suit. However, it's interesting to note that Cubase SX3 has partly returned to its roots and now offers a more pattern-orientated way of working, with the inclusion of the new Play Order track. Once again, musicians can move verses, choruses and other relevant sections of their songs around. Great stuff, but why did the company wait so long?

Tech terms

Real-time recording

A process which can be conducted while the sequencer is actually running. For example, tempo changes recorded using a MIDI controller would be done in real time, without stopping the program.

Step input

A method of entering MIDI note data into a song, either with the mouse or using a MIDI keyboard, while the sequencer is stopped.

Resolution

A sequencer's smallest unit of time (tick) that's possible within a bar. For example, in Logic this is 1/3,840. Some people refer to resolution as 'pulses per quarter note' (PPQ). In those terms, Logic's resolution is 960PPQ (3,840 divided by 4).

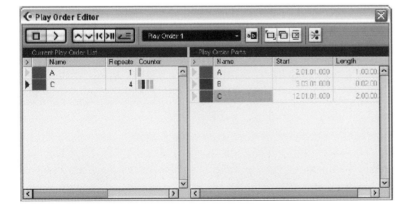

The new Play Order track in Cubase SX3 marks a return to the pattern-based approach to sequencing last seen in its ancestor, Pro24.

Cubase SX provides a 'staircase' icon for activating Step Input mode. Logic provides a keyboard window for step-inputting notes.

Maybe Steinberg is responding to the success of FL Studio (yes, Fruityloops has grown up). FL Studio is a pattern-based and step-entry sequencer combined. Patterns can be welded together using a playlist. And, just like the Play Order tracks in SX3, FL's playlist also supports audio tracks (audio is streamed from the computer's hard drive).

All aboard

With the success of Notator and Cubase, Atari computers were popping up in commercial studios everywhere. However, not everybody was computer savvy and before long sequencers were being installed in hardware synthesizers such as the M1, which featured an onboard 8-track sequencer capable of holding ten songs and 100 patterns. So good was the M1 at that time that entire backing tracks were sequenced using only the onboard sounds.

Korg has continued the tradition to this day and its Triton range of synths all feature 16-track onboard sequencers, with cue lists for arranging patterns and facilities for both real-time and step-entry recording. The Triton Karma, in particular, is rather special. It features Kay Algorithmic Realtime Music Architecture (KARMA), a MIDI data-generating technology that takes input notes and controller movements and generates complex musical phrases and effects. For anybody who owns a Korg Karma, special editing software written by Stephen Kay, the inventor of KARMA, is available for PC and Mac. And that brings us neatly to another type of sequencing software.

The generation game

Apart from just recording data and editing it, sequencers can be put to work in other, more creative, ways. Mathematicians often make good musicians and vice versa, and ever since the Atari days, musical boffins have been producing fractal music-composition software. FractMus 2000 – a freeware download (PC), by the way – is one such program. It generates notes and melodies using 12 algorithms from – wait for it – number theory, chaotic dynamics, fractals and cellular automata.

A similar program, called MusicWonk (yes, that is spelt correctly), also generates algorithmic MIDI music and, if you're the experimental type, provides you with an opportunity to create riffs based on non-traditional patterns. It'll generate tunes from such unlikely sources as DNA sequences, stock market trends, star maps and any other algorithmic data source you care to throw at it. MusicWonk's big brother, ArtWonk, not only produces MIDI music, but graphic animation too, also based on algorithmic processes.

Of course, sequencers such as these will not actually generate complete compositions (not yet, anyway), but saving the results as MIDI files and importing them into notation software or a conventional sequencer can provide an almost inexhaustible source of melodic material to work with.

Audio young dudes

In response to the growing popularity of loop-based music production, a few years ago several 'audio only' sequencers appeared on the market. Ableton Live, for example, provided facilities for mixing and matching samples of any tempo and pitch. Several other popular audio sequencers, such as Fruityloops and Acid, did much the same thing. These easy-to-use sequencers were – and still are – extremely popular and attracted a new generation to computer music making. However, these programs appear to be growing up and now, depending on which version you buy, include some degree of MIDI functionality.

Sequencing software such as Fruityloops may have made sequencing easy, but it was Apple that brought it to the masses, with GarageBand. Free with all new Macs, GarageBand is a versatile entry-level sequencer suitable for recording audio and basic MIDI sequencing. However, it's as an audio loop-production tool that it really excels and Apple provides thousands of loops, packaged as Jam Packs, to use with the software.

Cool Edit Pro, yet another loop-based sequencer, was recently acquired by Adobe, given a makeover and re-branded as Adobe Audition. With its ability to exchange files with Premier Pro and After Effects, Adobe is aiming the new sequencer at video professionals who need to knock up quick-and-easy soundtracks. But is that such a good thing? It's doubtful that many musicians and composers would think so. Except one perhaps – if he was still alive. Maybe, 50 years on, Raymond Scott's dream of a sequencer that composes automatically is nearing reality after all.

Adobe Audition is Cool Edit Pro given a makeover. This powerful sequencing suite is aimed at video professionals involved in writing and recording soundtracks, as evident from its close associations with Premier Pro.

Further info

This page displays a photo of Raymond Scott's Wall Of Sound (arguably the world's first sequencer). Follow the links and you'll be reading for hours.
www.intuitivemusic.com/tguidesequencer.html
Excellent site devoted to Raymond Scott, an unsung genius (until now).
http://raymondscott.com
Tim Conrardy's fascinating Vintage Sequencer pages. But that's not all – check out the other pages on the menu.
www.tweakheadz.com/vintage_sequencers.html

30

Stereo

Of all the skills and techniques an engineer possesses, the know-how and ability to arrange two microphones and create an accurate stereo recording should never be undervalued. But for many, the full extent of the various methods remains largely unexplored.

Stereo recording has been around since the 30s (although it took a while for domestic replay systems to catch up), yet it is still the principal method by which music is recorded and replayed. Here, we're going to explore the ins and outs of some of these techniques.

Choosing your mics

If you're recording an acoustically balanced ensemble, opting for a simple stereo mic configuration always delivers the best results. With contemporary recorded music, mono close-mics tend to be the preferred option, although the addition of true stereo elements can widen the depth and detail in any track.

The most important ingredients of a good stereo recording are two matched condenser microphones, although finding the right position and arrangement is crucial to getting the best results. Different arrangements yield differing amounts of reflected sound (otherwise known as reverb or ambience), wider soundstages, better or worse mono compatibility, and in some cases demand different ideal replay equipment. Deciding which of these factors is important to your recording will inform your selections from the various available options.

How we perceive stereo

Before we delve too deeply into the various positions available, it's worth considering how we hear and perceive stereo information. The ear principally uses two approaches to decoding a stereo image – timing and amplitude. An instrument placed at the far left of the soundstage will reach the left ear before it reaches the right – the brain decodes this timing deviation as a left placement.

Alongside this timing information there will also be an amplitude discrepancy caused by your head absorbing high-frequency sound and 'ghosting' out part of the image. This partly explains the omni-directionality of bass and why our left/right perception of high-frequency sounds is far more defined.

Coincident pair

The classic stereo pair configuration involves two directional mics (eg. cardioid or hyper-cardioid) placed relatively close to one another (ideally the capsules should be aligned one on top of the other) at an angle of 90-130° to each other. This setup – called a 'coincident pair' – was developed by the godfather of stereo recording Alan Blumlein, and uses the amplitude discrepancy of signals picked up by the left and right mics to define the stereo sound.

Coincident pairs (also known as 'XY pairs') provide a defined, natural stereo image and – given the proximity of the mics to each other – few phase problems. A particular strength (or weakness) is their rejection of sound coming from the rear, which is a good way of controlling excess reverb or unwanted noise in the recording, such as the audience at a gig.

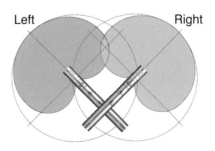

Coincident pair: the most common stereo arrangement produces an accurate stereo image with no phase problems.

Spaced pair

The principal alternative to a coincident arrangement is the 'spaced pair', usually employing two omni-directional microphones placed a metre or so apart. Whereas coincident pairs take advantage of the differences in amplitude between the two mics, the spaced pair technique uses the timing differential between the signals, and it produces a wide, flattering stereo image.

The use of the omni-directional pattern yields a very flat frequency response (by comparison with other directional patterns), which works well given the objective of trying to capture a natural sound. Having a 360° pickup also means that the microphones will pick up plenty of natural ambience, which is sometimes desirable if the recording is taking place in a nice-sounding room or hall.

Spaced-omni configuration: provides a wide stereo image, working principally from timing differences between sounds arriving at either microphone.

The spacing of the mics is the key to defining the width of the recording – with a spaced pair offering the widest possible sound of all the techniques being discussed. For most conventional sound sources, a distance of one metre between mics will be sufficient, although they can easily be spaced up to half the width of the soundstage for particularly wide sound sources.

The downside of the increased width offered by spaced omnis is the hole that can begin to appear in the centre of the stereo image (a similar result can occur in a mix when too many signals are panned hard left and right). Because of the timing differences between channels, if the recording is summed to mono, phase problems will also appear.

Near-coincident arrangement: captures both amplitude and timing differences.

Near-coincident pair

A possible compromise between the two extremes of coincident pairs and spaced pairs is the 'near-coincident' arrangement. This setup uses a combination of the two techniques, so the microphones are slightly spaced apart – no more than about 50 centimetres – but retain the relative angle and polar patterns of the coincident arrangement. The use of near-coincident mics creates an effective balance between the amplitude differences highlighted by a coincident pair, and the timing differences captured by the spaced pair – making the technique akin to how the human ear works.

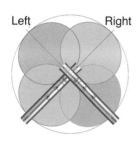

The Blumlein technique: is a variation on the coincident theme – use two figure-of-8 microphones to create a complete 360° pickup.

Using a figure-of-8 mic

So far, the examples we've investigated have used mics with two polar patterns – cardioid and omni-directional. But there is another pattern that's particularly useful for stereo recording: it's called the 'figure-of-8'. These microphones are bi-directional – in other words, they pick up sound from the front and rear, but reject sound coming from the side.

For most conventional recording tasks a figure-of-8 microphone is of limited use, but in a stereo combination it can be used to create a 'crossed bi-directional pair' or a 'middle-and-side' (M/S) pair. If you're considering buying a matched pair of mics for stereo recording, check that they include a figure-of-8 polar position, as many budget condensers omit this as a means of cutting costs.

A crossed bi-directional pair, also known as the Blumlein technique, uses two figure-of-8 capsules, placed on top of one another and angled at 90°. This technique is essentially an earlier version of the coincident pair (initially Blumlein only had omni- and bi-directional mics to work with), offering the same accurate stereo image, with the added advantage of a complete 360° pickup pattern. The Blumlein technique is an ideal choice for capturing ambient sound as well as direct sound, without the potential for phase problems and stereo 'holes' of spaced omnis.

Middle-and-side

The middle-and-side (M/S) technique uses the figure-of-8 polar pattern again, in another form of the coincident arrangement. A potential deterrent for some users is that the recordings require decoding – it's also what makes M/S unique by offering greater control and flexibility after the recording session. The distinguishing feature of the M/S technique (and the reason it's so popular among broadcast and film sound recordists) lies in its ability to deliver an accurate on-axis mono image, alongside a controllable stereo width element – all from just two microphones.

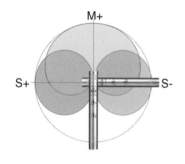

Middle-and-side pair: provides a solid on-axis mono image as well a controllable stereo width. The recordings will need decoding before you can hear the results.

In an M/S configuration, a cardioid mic will be used, pointing directly at the sound source to form the middle (or M) signal. The figure-of-8 microphone is then arranged at 90° to the middle microphones, to form the side component (or S signal). The two signals will then be tracked, onto two tracks of a suitable recorder as usual, but will need to be decoded to form the final stereo image.

Decoding the recordings involves splitting out the S signal onto two adjacent channels, panned hard left and right, with one channel phase inverted. With the middle signal panned centrally, bring the two side channels up – as you do this, the perceived width of the recording should increase accordingly. If you're pushed for channels, an M/S decoder plug-in (such as Logic's DirMixer) can decode the signals.

Other techniques

Soundfield microphones offer an expensive but highly configurable approach to stereo recording. Developed from the principles of M/S recording, the soundfield microphone uses a total of four cardioid capsules, all packed inside a single microphone case. The accompanying converter unit decodes the array of capsules into a series of possible images, offering complete control of the width and depth of the image across a full 360º. Unlike M/S decoding, you'll need to allow four spare tracks (one per capsule) if you want the full range of decoding options later on.

Binaural setups represent the logical conclusion to stereo recording by replicating our perception of the stereo image. The technique uses two – ideally small – omni-directional mics that are placed either side of a dummy (or real!) head. Configured in this way, the recording captures a completely accurate document of the timing discrepancies and (by the addition of the head as a sound absorber) the amplitude discrepancies. The only thing preventing this from being the perfect system for stereo recording is that to fully appreciate the qualities binaural captures requires the listener to use headphones rather than loudspeakers. Reassuringly, despite all the advances in 5.1 and other multi-speaker surround sound systems, listening to a true binaural recording on headphones remains a stunning experience.

Conclusions

In the increasingly complex world of music and recording, it's easy to forget that the most direct, emotionally effective tracks come from a very simple combination of elements. Whether you're just starting out in the world of recording or are a seasoned pro, why not take some time to explore the simple delights of a stereo recording – no overdubs, no complicated mix, just great music.

Further info

For more information on stereo recording techniques visit
www.tape.com/Bartlett_Articles/stereo_microphone_techniques.html
www.fullcompass.com/fyi/default.aspx?pgid=77
www.kellyindustries.com/microphones/stereo_miking_techniques.html
A brief history of stereophonic sound can be found at
http://history.acusd.edu/gen/recording/stereo.html
The life and work of Alan Blumlein, godfather of stereo, can be found at
www.doramusic.com
For more information on the world of binaural recording, pay a visit to
www.binaural.com
To hear some fascinating binaural sound works by Dallas Simpson
www.waterpump.f9.co.uk

Manufacturers' sites
www.akg.com
www.neumann.com
www.soundfield.com

Tech terms

Condenser microphone
Condenser microphones use two electrically charged diaphragms to convert sound energy into electrical energy. Their wide frequency response and sensitivity to even the quietest of sounds make them ideal for stereo recording.

Polar pattern
Polar patterns differentiate the various directional characteristics of a given microphone. Having a variety of polar patterns, as often found on condenser microphones, is essential for exploring a range of stereo recording techniques.

Cardioid
A cardioid polar response has a distinctive heart-shaped pickup response pattern, so it attenuates sound coming from the rear of the microphone.

Hypercardioid
Hypercardioid microphones have a tighter front pickup pattern than cardioids, and a small amount of rear sensitivity.

String synths and samplers

Musicians and record producers have been using the string orchestra to augment the traditional rock group line-up of guitars, bass and drums since the 1950s. Until the mid-60s, the rockers and rollers of the day would play alongside the gentlemen of the orchestra in the same studio because everything was recorded in one take to two-track stereo.

Mello-traumatic

With the advent of multitrack recording, rock musicians decided to add 'strings' to their records themselves, using electronic keyboard instruments such as the Mellotron. This extraordinary contraption was notoriously unreliable, which is not surprising really because each note on the keyboard had its own two-metre length of tape, which played back the sounds of pre-recorded violins and cellos for up to eight seconds.

Arguably the forerunner to the modern sampler, it was a favourite with The Beatles and The Moody Blues, who used it on just about every song they recorded in the 70s. Jean Michel Jarre still uses his Mellotron. Rick Wakeman burnt his, allegedly.

Strings in a box

By the mid-70s dedicated string machines arrived on the scene, the most famous being the ARP Solina String Ensemble. Using cheap, electronic organ technology, it was renowned for its warm, lush sound, achieved with sophisticated built-in chorus circuitry. Goodness knows what it would have sounded like without it. Used by the Eagles and Elton John and featured on numerous disco hits, it didn't sound anything like a real string orchestra, but was suitable for background pads or slow-moving melody lines.

Enter the sampler

Things changed in the 80s and 90s with the birth of digital sampling technology. For the first time, musicians could write and record complete orchestral arrangements using samplers like the Akai 1000. Using an Atari computer, a sampler and a sequencer, musicians could now add the sound of real strings to their songs.

In the early 90s E-MU Systems took things a stage further and used their high-end sampler, the Emulator 3, to record a realistic set of string samples and stored them as onboard ROM in the Proteus/2 Orchestral sound mod-

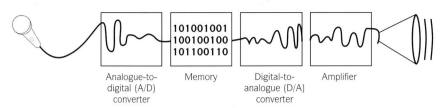

During the sampling process analogue sound information is converted to digital information and stored in the memory of a computer or sampler. The process is reversed on playback.

Analogue-to-digital (A/D) converter   Memory   Digital-to-analogue (D/A) converter   Amplifier

ule. An updated version is still available now under the name of the Virtuoso 2000, and it provides a quick and easy way to knock up a realistic string orchestra.

As a concept the sampling process is very simple. For example, a single violin or a complete string section makes a sound that strikes the diaphragm of a microphone and a corresponding voltage is generated. Analogue-to-digital converters measure the voltage, converting it to a number that can be stored in digital memory. To play back the sound, the numbers are converted to voltages again by a digital-to-analogue converter. Finally they're amplified and sent to a speaker, which converts the voltages to sound waves.

Meet the orchestra

Before you embark on writing string arrangements it's important to get to know the instruments themselves; how they're played, their sound characteristics, their playing range and so on.

The string orchestra consists of four sections, covering the complete musical spectrum – soprano, alto, tenor and bass (SATB). Violins usually carry the melody and cover the high, soprano range. They're usually divided into two sections – violins 1 and violins 2. A safe, practical working range for the violin section is from G2 (the lowest open string) to about C6 on a MIDI keyboard. When played in the high register, the second violins are often used to double the line at the octave below, to provide strength and cohesion.

Violas cover the mid, or alto range and are darker in character than the violins. A safe working range for the viola is C2 to about C5 on a MIDI keyboard. It's used mainly to provide the inner harmonies of a chord, and can be divided into sub-groups for this purpose. Viola players are rarely featured and other musicians frequently tell 'viola' jokes behind their backs (all in good fun, of course).

HALion String Edition is a VST instrument, sample player and sample library, all in one package.

Tech terms

Legato

Connected notes without gaps between them. Strictly speaking, all notes are played with one stroke of the bow, without changing the direction of the bow. In a string section all the players change their bowing direction at different times.

Pizzicato

The player plucks the strings with the fingers. The higher the note, the thinner the sound.

Spiccato

Often confused with pizzicato, but actually completely different. The bow is bounced on the strings to produce short, fast-decaying notes, often used in fast passages.

Tremolo

Rapid back and forth strokes of the bow are used to create a sense of urgency and anticipation.

Cellos cover the lower ranges. They're strong and powerful in their low, baritone range, and expressive when played in their higher, tenor range. They're sometimes used to carry the melody. A comfortable playing range is from C1 to G4.

Double basses, of course, cover the bass range and frequently double the cellos at an octave below, for extra strength. Their playing range is C0 to C3, but they rarely go very high.

Painting by numbers

For many musicians, the cheapest and easiest way to re-create strings is to use a General MIDI sound module like the Roland Sound Canvas. Used carefully they can provide a pretty convincing string orchestra mock-up. The basic GM sound-set contains individual instruments starting with violin, at program number 41, through to double bass at 44. The quality varies considerably depending on the manufacturer, but generally speaking, they don't sound too realistic.

Far better are the ensemble strings at program number 49. Using just this program will produce a decent all-round string orchestra from violins to double basses. Strings 2, at program number 50, generally have slower attack times and are better for slower passages. Programs 51 and 52, usually named Synth Strings 1 and 2, are more synthetic in character and better suited to keyboard-style pads and backgrounds. Program number 45 contains tremolo strings, an eerie effect produced by short, rapid back-and-forth bow movements near the bridge. Number 46 houses the pizzicato strings, the sound of players plucking the strings with their fingers.

The HALion way

Many film composers write their string scores using a sequencer like Logic and a high-end sample library, before actually recording the real orchestra. Unfortunately, most of these libraries come with a fairly hefty price tag. However, with a moderately powerful computer and the HALion String Edition Vol.1, you can do the same. It was developed by Wizoo as a tool for arrangers and composers orchestrating their scores on a budget and is supplied with eight CDs full of very useable, high-quality string samples.

The beauty of a sampler player such as this is that much of the hard work has been done for you, with a variety of bowing styles and articulations on offer to help create authentic-sounding parts. Legato, pizzicato, spiccato, tremolo and trills are all there. For beginners, special 'four-in-one' programs are included, where all four sections (violins, violas, cellos and basses) are combined into one. Of course, that is a compromise, but once mixed into the background (as they usually are) only the trained ear will spot the difference.

Keep it simple

Scoring strings can be a daunting task for the beginner. Listen to recordings and read books on the subject, but don't allow a lack of technique to prevent you getting started. String sections are in vogue at the moment and feature on quite a few recent chart hits, but listen closely and you'll discover that more often than not a single melody line is all that's necessary. As a rule of thumb, keep it simple behind the vocal with flowing lines and leave the flowery bits for filling gaps and maybe solos.

Shaping and scraping

If you're into creating and programming analogue synths and you're not too concerned about authenticity, it's fairly easy to create string sounds. Choosing the correct waveform to begin with is crucial, and sawtooth waveforms are best for synthesising strings.

Shaping the amplifier envelope is just as important. As you probably know, string players (sometimes unkindly referred to as 'scrapers') produce a sound by striking a string with their bow and then drawing it back and forth across the string. The attack, decay, sustain and release controls of the synthesizer's volume envelope should ideally reflect the way you want your virtual player to behave. For example, the harder a string is initially struck, the shorter the envelope's attack time will need to be.

A typical string patch for normal bowing would have moderate attack, decay and release times (knobs around 12 o'clock), and sustain set at its highest level. As the synthesizer's key is pressed, there's a slight crescendo at the beginning of the note due to the moderately slow attack time. If you lengthen the decay (say, set the knob at 3 o'clock) and reduce the sustain level (to 9 o'clock), the note will drop in level after the initial attack time. This too is a fairly common and natural sound.

If you were to set the sustain level to its minimum level, only the attack and decay will be heard – holding down the key has no effect. Moving the attack setting to its shortest possible time and setting the decay at 12 o'clock produces a plucked pizzicato sound.

If you have a copy of Cubase SX, you can easily re-create the classic sound of the Solina String Ensemble by using the A1 synth. It's found as a preset in the Pad section. Two oscillators are used to create sawtooth waveforms, which are treated heavily with a chorus effect, just like the original.

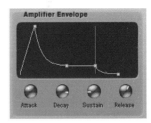

A longer decay and reduced sustain level produces natural fade after the initial attack of a note.

A typical string patch will include moderate attack, decay and release times.

Minimum sustain levels and short attack times produce a plucked pizzicato sound.

Further info

Books
Orchestral Technique by Gordon Jacob, pub. Oxford University Press.
Online guides
http://emusician.com/ar/emusic_creating_realistic_ensembles
www.petethomas.co.uk/composition-arranging/strings.html
String samplers online
www.steinberg.net/en/products/vst_instruments/halion_strings/index.php?sid=0
www.emu.com/products/product.asp?product=1086&category=627&maincategory=627
String Sample Libraries online
www.soniccontrol.com/tech/midi/articles/samplecds/sistrings.shtml
www.garritan.com

Surround sound

It's widely accepted that surround sound is a more realistic listening experience than any of its predecessors, and everyone from the Hollywood filmmaker to the bedroom sound engineer is buying into the fact that surround format recording and reproduction is here to stay. But with an ever-developing array of formats and standards it becomes increasingly difficult to know where to start.

What is 5.1?

Most of us have heard the term '5.1' before; but what exactly is it? At the moment, 5.1 is the standard surround format for motion picture, music and digital television. The format consists of six channels of audio that resolve in a six-speaker configuration. Three speakers are placed in front of the listener and are called (and positioned) 'Left', 'Right' and 'Centre' (L, R and C); two speakers are placed behind the listener – these are generally called 'Left surround' and 'Right surround' (or Ls and Rs). The sixth speaker is a subwoofer (the LFE speaker) that's often placed behind the three speakers at the front. The sixth channel has only a narrow frequency response (3Hz to 120Hz), thus it is sometimes referred to as the '.1' channel. When put together, the system is usually referred to as having 5.1 channels.

A brief history of surround

Sound engineers began experimenting with surround sound formats while our grandparents were fighting World War II. In 1941, Walt Disney's Fantasia was released with a classical music soundtrack that was recorded on four discrete tracks made up of separate sections of the orchestra. The surround system consisted of one speaker in each corner of the cinema; the idea was to make it sound like instruments were moving around the room and this was achieved by the way the music was mixed. This first type of surround sound was dubbed 'Fantasound' and it was reasonably impressive – especially when you consider that most recordings made before 1950 are mono! Unfortunately, Fantasound didn't catch on, mainly due to expense – the audio had to be played in sync with the picture, but from a separate reel, meaning extra equipment.

By the late 1950s, Hollywood films were being encoded with simpler multi-channel formats. These used four or more analogue magnetic audio tracks around the edges of the film. Magnetic tracks could not produce as clear a sound as the conventional optical audio tracks, and they tended to fade with time, but they took up a lot less space on the film. The standard film format didn't have enough room for more than two optical tracks, but it was possible to squeeze as many as six magnetic tracks around the film frame; these consisted of the more familiar left, right, centre and surround channels.

In the 1970s and 1980s Dolby Laboratories developed various surround formats and we saw the addition of the subwoofer channel. The early 1990s witnessed the introduction of digital surround sound systems that worked with an external digital playback device, such as a CD player, that was sync'ed to the picture with a timecode. Later developments, such as the Dolby Digital format, put the multi-channel signals back on the film edge as digital code. These later formats use the L, R, C, Ls, Rs and LFE configuration that we know as 5.1.

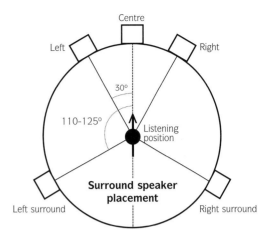

The standard 5.1 speaker configuration. Note that the equilateral triangular listening position for stereo listening is still present.

Where is 5.1 used?

There are many different applications for 5.1 sound, and although film post-production is still the main area of surround mixing, it won't be long before every man and his dog is geared up to receive and play multi-channel sound formats. This will open the door to more music, TV and possibly radio arriving in our homes – or cars – in 5.1.

DVD music videos are becoming popular for music mixed in surround, and music for films is being recorded and mixed directly in 5.1 before it even reaches the dubbing stage of film post-production. Sound designers working in the computer games industry are also creating games in surround sound formats.

Setting up for surround

When it comes to setting up your studio to work in 5.1, you first need to upgrade to six-speaker monitoring. Although it's ideal to have five identical speakers and a sub, you can always just add to your existing monitors.

You'll also need to think about amplification. Most pro surround monitors are active, enabling the engineer to output directly from his desk or computer. If your monitoring is passive, you'll need to invest in either a multi-channel amplifier or three stereo amplifiers to give you your six channels.

Whatever software you use to create your sound, you'll need a soundcard or interface with at least six outputs. There are plenty of affordable soundcards on the market that are specifically designed for outputting 5.1, but it's worth making sure they're compatible with the software you're using.

If you're serious about making surround sound mixes, you should consider using a Bass Manager. This is a piece of hardware that sits between your output and the speakers; it collects all the frequencies below 80Hz from all channels and sends them directly to the LFE speaker. The reason it's important to do this when mixing is that most consumer surround systems contain bass management; if you don't mix with one, then you're not hearing it the way people will listen at home.

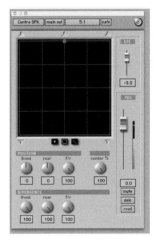

The surround panner enables free movement of signals between all the main speakers. You can see that the LFE send is an auxiliary send on the right-hand side of the channel.

Tech terms

LFE

Low Frequency Enhancement. The sub-woofer channel in the surround sound config-uration.

dBFS

Decibels Full Scale. This is a digital scale relating to bit depth, where 0dB is your highest bit and the limit of your dynam-ic range. So 0dBFS is the loudest signal you can record in a digital recorder before clipping occurs.

Bass Manager

A device that redirects low-frequency sound from the five main sur-round channels to the LFE channel.

Control room configuration

Accurate positioning of your monitors will help you get the best surround image. The five main speakers should be positioned to create a circle, the centre of which will be the optimum listening position (see the diagram). The front of each speaker will sit on the circumference of the circle facing towards the listener. The left and right speakers still form the equilateral triangle that's recommended for stereo listening, with the centre speaker placed between them. The position of the rear speakers can vary slightly, but gen-erally should be at an angle between 110 and 125 degrees from the middle of the centre speaker.

Positioning the subwoofer is a bit of a black art, but you should place it outside the circle. Low frequencies are less directional, which is why there's no strict position for the subwoofer. One favoured location is behind the for-ward three speakers, but try moving it from behind the front speakers to the sides and decide where it sounds best. You should also experiment with which way it faces.

Software and hardware

The beauty of using hardware or software that's geared up for surround is the inclusion of a 'surround panner'. This type of pan control is usually repre-sented by a joystick control; it enables you to move the sound between the five speakers. In addition to the five main speakers, the send to the LFE should be an auxiliary type because it's used to 'enhance' the main signals. Most modern sequencers include 5.1 capability, including Pro Tools, Nuendo and Cubase SX.

Even if you don't have specifically 5.1-capable software, all you really need to mix in surround (apart from the speakers) is at least six discreet out-puts from your recording system. If you're using a conventional mixing desk in your setup, you need six discreet outputs – these can be in the form of main outputs, sub outputs or busses – and a single auxiliary for the LFE.

Recording for surround

There are very few changes in the way music is recorded for surround because most of the 'magic' takes place in the mixdown; mono or stereo recordings are panned into position (or sent to the LFE) later in the process. There are engineers out there pioneering 'surround' mic'ing techniques, and a lot of progress has been made in this area with classical orchestral recordings.

Alongside traditional mic'ing techniques, the addition of ambient micro-phones positioned around an instrument (or band) in a fashion that mimics the arrangement of the five main monitoring speakers enables the engineer to create a surround image of the sound being recorded by panning the channels to the corresponding speakers. This technique can be applied to most instruments, but it does rely heavily on the sound of the recording space. If you're limited by physical space or equipment, the best policy is to 'create' the surround environment at the mixdown by positioning the instru-ments and effect returns in the surround image.

Mixing in surround

Mixing in surround is the fun part. You can create fantastic results with even the simplest techniques, such as sending reverb on sounds to the rear speakers to create greater perspective, or placing your main vocal in the centre speaker to make the stereo image less cluttered and the vocals clearer. The possibilities are endless.

The surround panner function is a great tool for moving sounds between speakers in real time. Software that includes a surround panner generally also has automation capability, enabling you to record the movements. Without this type of panner you can achieve the same type of movements by copying the sound you want to move on two identical tracks assigned to different speakers and crossfading between them. If you want to make a sound that's moving from speaker to speaker appear to be moving away from the listener, try a Doppler-type effect on the end of the sound for added realism. But the main thing is to experiment and have fun!

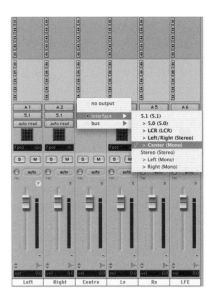

Pro Tools' 5.1 mixer includes dedicated outputs for mixing in surround formats.

Converting 5.1 mixes to stereo

Once you've mixed down in 5.1, you can convert the mix to stereo by using a technique called 'folding down'. The principle is to add the outputs together at different levels; any movement you have between speakers will still be preserved to some extent. See the table above for how to fold down.

The sonic revolution

It won't be long before surround sound becomes a (if not, the) major format for music applications. As home 5.1 becomes more affordable, domestic users will want to use their home cinema systems to listen to music in surround as well as just watching movies. Consumers will soon be able to buy albums that include interviews, videos and an entire back catalogue of previous work, all on one disc and all at high resolution with audio quality exceeding the limited 16-bit/44.1kHz of standard CD. It's time for all of us to start considering how we're going to take advantage of this exciting format.

Further info

If you want to investigate the way surround sound is implemented and reproduced in the theatre, check out these sites:

www.dolby.com

http://entertainment.howstuffworks.com/surround-sound.htm

For a more serious guide to surround sound, geared towards setting up your studio for producing 5.1 sound for music, television and the cinema look up this title:

5.1 Surround Sound Up and Running, by: Tomlinson Holman, Focal Press, ISBN: 0-240-80383-3

The *Surround Professional* magazine website contains articles and technical information for engineers, producers and sound designers

www.surroundpro.com

Synchronisation

Are you one of the increasing numbers of computer-based musicians who are chasing the sound-to-picture market? If so, sooner or later you'll find yourself confronting the seemingly complicated issue of synchronisation and all the bewildering acronyms that go with the subject – LTC, VITC, MTC and all the rest.

For many, writing the music is the easy bit. The difficult part is getting everything hooked up so that your music exactly fits the director's video frames. Split-second timing and rock solid synchronisation is essential.

Even if you're not interested in becoming the next Hans Zimmer, you may well need to synchronise computer-generated MIDI tracks with an external audio recorder. For devices such as audio recorders, video decks and sequencers to be considered synchronised, they must run together at exactly the same time and tempo. And in order to do that, one of them – the 'master' – must dictate the tempo to the others – the 'slaves'.

Role play

For example, you might set up a video recorder to transmit timecode to a sequencer like Cubase. In that case, Cubase would be the slave and the video recorder the master. Of course, you could just as easily set them up the opposite way around, with Cubase as the master. Furthermore, you could have Cubase act as both master and slave by having it transmit MIDI Clock to a drum machine, while simultaneously receiving timecode from the video recorder. But what exactly is MIDI Clock and timecode, and what's the difference between them? First a little history…

Impulsive behaviour

Back in the 80s, before MIDI came along, electro musicians used to synchronise their analogue sequencers and drum machines by sending regularly spaced electrical impulses (Pulse Clock) from one to the other. Before long, a method of encoding these impulses known as Frequency Shift Keying (FSK) code was developed and boffins in studios across the land were 'slaving' their beat boxes to tape recorders.

Unfortunately, FSK had no position indicator, and you always had to start at the beginning of a song (no intros or outros). Once MIDI arrived on the scene, FSK was soon replaced by MIDI Clock, a tempo-based synchronisation signal.

Used in conjunction with Song Position Pointer (SPP), a master device could now send 24 MIDI Clock messages for every quarter note (12 for every eighth note, and so on) and our electro musicians could now start and stop

You can route MIDI tracks to VST instruments running on another computer using Cubase SX and VST System Link.

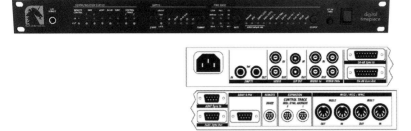

A glance at the Digital Timepiece rear panel shows connections for ADAT (Alesis) and DA-88 (Tascam) and Sony synchronisation protocols, as well as the usual MTC, MMC, SMPTE and Word Clock.

their drum machines anywhere within a song and vary the tempo. All modern devices still use this system of tempo-based synchronisation.

Naming and framing

With the demise of FSK, the recording industry adopted a method of synchronisation used in the film world and began 'striping' analogue tape with SMPTE timecode. Laid down as a standard for encoding film frames by the Society of Motion Picture and Television Engineers, SMPTE (pronounced 'simptee') sends a 24-hour clock-type synchronisation message related to hours, minutes, seconds and frames (divisions of a second). With SMPTE, seconds are not divided into tenths and hundredths, but into frames.

You might have seen the abbreviation 'EBU'. It's exactly the same timecode as SMPTE and was renamed by the European Broadcasting Union when they adopted it for use with European frame rates.

As with most synchronisation formats, nothing's ever perfect. Because of the differing alternating current frequencies between continents (USA: 60Hz – Europe: 50Hz), so the frame rates also vary and 24, 25 and 30fps (frames per second) are now in common use. For this reason, when you connect up a series of devices they must all be set to identical frame rates.

In Cubase SX Timecode and Machine Control are managed in the Synchronization Setup window.

Types of timecode

There are three main types of timecode. VITC (Vertical Interval Time Code – pronounced 'vitzee') is a video format, stored in the actual visual images. MTC (MIDI Time Code) is a translation of SMPTE, which is transmitted via a MIDI cable. LTC (Longitudinal Time Code) is another name for SMPTE/EBU and is recorded onto the audio tracks of both audio and video recorders.

Although LTC can be output from an audio recorder during fast-forwarding and rewinding, it can only be output from a video recorder at the normal playback speed. Obviously this isn't a satisfactory state of affairs when adding frame-synchronised music to the picture. To do that, you need a synchroniser like Emagic's Unitor8 that reads VITC. In fact, it reads and writes both LTC and VITC so it's good for both audio and video work.

Sound-to-picture professionals generally use a hardware synchroniser, such as Emagic's Unitor8, Nuendo Time Base (the first pro synchroniser to support VST System Link) or the MOTU Digital Timepiece. These machines will read and write all the different forms of timecode and synchronise most digital audio equipment with precision.

Tech terms

Drop-frame dfps

A type of SMPTE time-code used in the US for colour video production. Every minute (except the 10th minute), two frames are dropped to match the 'clock on the wall'.

Striping

When SMPTE timecode is recorded to tape as an audio signal, recording engineers refer to the process as 'striping' the tape.

Sync track

A track reserved on a multitrack audio recorder for SMPTE timecode.

TDIF

Tascam Digital Interface. A protocol for sending digital signals to and from Tascam multitrack recorders, such as the DA-88.

S/PDIF

Sony/Philips Digital Interface. Uses either coaxial cable with RCA connectors or optical cable with Toslink connectors.

Talking clock

If you happen to work in a completely virtual environment, you'll never need to worry about external synchronisation, but it is, of course, happening in the background. Audio, MIDI and video are synchronised by your computer's very own digital audio clock. It's usually very stable, but this stability is threatened when you use external timecode synchronisation.

Although your sequencer and recorded audio tracks play back in perfect sync (because you're using the computer's clock), there's no guarantee that the system synchronised to timecode (your video or audio tape and MIDI equipment) will do the same. There is room for drift. What's needed is a single master clock, to control the whole system.

Word Clock is purely a timing reference for digital audio devices and is really just a replacement for the sample rate clock in your audio card. It doesn't carry any timecode information and can't be used to synchronise devices on its own. It can, however, provide a common timing reference to multiple devices, enabling them to be synchronised with one another. Devices that use Word Clock include digital mixers, standalone hard disk recorders, computer-based digital audio workstations and computer audio cards.

Apart from using Word Clock to stabilise a synchronisation setup, you can also use it when making digital transfers. For example, to make a transfer between certain digital audio devices – for example, a MOTU 2408 audio interface and a digital mixer – they must be connected via Word Clock cables. Doing so will ensure that both devices are synchronised to the same rate of digital audio, enabling consistent playback. In fact, the combination of SMPTE and Word Clock is the ideal sync scenario.

A typical synchronisation setup for sound-to-picture might look like the diagram above. A video recorder is sending LTC or VITC to a synchroniser, which in turn feeds Word Clock to a computer (running Cubase or Logic) and MIDI timecode to a MIDI interface (connected to the computer).

Machine control

Yet another type of synchronisation, called MIDI Machine Control (MMC), enables you to control all your studio devices from a single MIDI source – usually a sequencer – by sending three simple messages: Play, Stop and Locate.

For example, you could have Cubase or Logic send an MMC Play message to a synchroniser like MOTU's MIDI Timepiece AV. The AV will respond to the message by generating and distributing timecode to all your linked devices, perhaps an ADAT (via an ADAT sync cable), a hard disk recorder (via MIDI cables), and the computer itself (via serial or parallel cables). And, of course, MIDI Machine Control can also be used to operate just a single device, such as a hard disk recorder.

Those clever folks at Steinberg have recently developed a network system for digital audio called VST System Link. It can be used to synchronise several computers without Ethernet cards, hubs or the usual paraphernalia associated with networking. You can use digital audio and MIDI cables instead, as long as each computer in the system is equipped with a suitable ASIO-compatible audio interface.

Using VST System Link you can do all manner of powerful things, such as

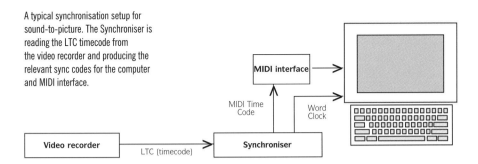

A typical synchronisation setup for sound-to-picture. The Synchroniser is reading the LTC timecode from the video recorder and producing the relevant sync codes for the computer and MIDI interface.

Frame rates

Frame rate	Application
24fps	35mm film
25fps	European video and audio (EBU)
29.97fps	Very rare
30fps	Audio in the US
29.97dfps	Video in US (Drop-frame code)

Info

A frame rate is the number of frames per second in a film or on a video tape. The type used depends on the application and the production location.

having one computer run your VST instruments, while another gets on with the task of recording your audio tracks. Or, if you needed extra audio tracks in a project, you could free up CPU on one computer and add the extra tracks to another machine.

Another possible scenario might be to set up a single computer to act as a virtual effects rack, and run all those CPU-intensive plug-ins we so dearly love to use. It's also a cross-platform system so you can take advantage of effect plug-ins and VST instruments that previously you could only use on either a Mac or a PC.

Wired for sound

Propellerhead Software's Rewire and Rewire2 protocols are another form of synchronisation and they provide sample-accurate audio synchronisation between programs such as Reason and Cubase SX/SL. Any two Rewire-compatible programs can share the same soundcard, transport controls and automatic and audio mixing controls. You can also route MIDI tracks from Cubase to Reason and control its various built-in synthesizers.

Further info

www.alesis.com/support/cc/sync.html
www.borg.com/~jglatt/tech/midispec/seq.htm
http://videoexpert.home.att.net/artic1/212smte.htm
www.fortunecity.com/tinpan/faithfull/379/mtc.html
Audio Post-production in Video and Film, Tim Amyes, Focal Press. ISBN 0240515420

Time and pitch

There are few things worse than hearing music being played out of time or out of tune – quite simply, it's painful listening! It's no surprise, therefore, that ever since musicians first started exploring recording technology, the need to modify both pitch and tempo has been paramount.

In the past, this kind of perfection was almost unobtainable, but now we have access to a wealth of tools which can 'fix' a bad performance. Whether it's time stretching, beat slicing or formant-preserving pitch shifting, they're all invaluable to the modern recording engineer.

However, although recent developments such as Apple Loops have finally made audio truly elastic, it's still worth differentiating between and understanding the various approaches available to you.

Getting up to speed

The simplest – and in many ways the most effective – way of modifying the tempo and pitch of a performance is to use varispeed. On a tape machine or a turntable, this simply means varying the speed of the motors that are moving the tape across the heads, or the speed at which the platter spins. In the digital world, a change in the sample rate (in other words, the rate at which sample data is read or recorded) again produces a varispeed effect, so a change in the Word Clock from 44.1kHz to 22.050kHz, for example, would produce half-speed playback.

Whichever medium you choose, the important factor to note is that varispeed adjusts both the pitch and the tempo, so a doubling of speed pro-

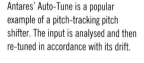

Antares' Auto-Tune is a popular example of a pitch-tracking pitch shifter. The input is analysed and then re-tuned in accordance with its drift.

duces an output that's one octave higher than the original recording. In most cases, this is fine – if you're beat-matching two records, for example – but in situations where you need to change just one aspect of the recording, varispeed is fatally flawed. What's more, as you move away from an instrument's natural pitch, the undesirable effect of 'munchkinisation' begins to rear its ugly head, but more on that later...

A bit shifty

If you need to alter tuning without affecting the duration of your input signal, pitch shifting is widely accepted as the best solution. Eventide introduced the concept of pitch shifting with its H910 Harmonizer in 1975, developed from a digital delay line. As with digital delay, the Harmonizer works by sampling audio into a buffer and replaying it to form the output signal. The difference, however, is that the Harmonizer's sample rate is altered between writing to and reading from this buffer, so as to create the transposed output.

More recently, the idea of pitch-tracking pitch shifters has enabled vocals (or any monophonic instrument) to be automatically re-tuned. These newer forms of pitch shifters analyse the incoming signal and compare it against the tunings of a pre-determined scale.

If a deviation is noted (–3 cents, for example), the pitch shifter will apply the corresponding inverse shift to pull the instrument or vocal back into line (in this case, +3 cents). If the tracking is set hard and the quantizing of the pitch is configured to tone or semitone steps, the tracking pitch-shifter produces the all-too-familiar Auto-Tune robotic vocal sound. If softer settings are used, the results can be surprisingly effective and go a long way to remedying a poor vocal take.

Time stretching – the reverse of pitch shifting, where the duration is changed without affecting pitch – first became widely available with the advent of digital samplers like the Akai S1000. As the process directly manipulates time, it is best employed as an off-line process. Time compression, for example, is conceptually impossible to achieve with anything other than a pre-recorded signal.

In essence, time stretching works in a similar way to granular synthesis, looping small segments of an input to extend its duration. Used carefully, it can be an effective way of achieving small shifts of tempo, but at extremes, the output of time stretching will sound increasingly grainy and metallic.

Recycling old for new

A more popular way of compressing or expanding rhythmic elements is beat slicing – best exemplified by Propellerhead's ReCycle. Here, the loop is analysed, cut up into bite-sized chunks and stored in a new .REX file format. These files can then be loaded into Reason's Dr.Rex loop player or another suitable audio program – Logic Pro, for example.

Unlike a conventional audio file, Dr.Rex can respond to the tempo of your track, either speeding up the slices or slowing them down to fit the given tempo.

Many other formats also follow the principles of beat slicing. Spectrasonics, as one example, had developed both its Groove Control system (which provides pre-cut loops along with associated MIDI files) and more

Tech terms

Off-line processing
Non-real-time processing carried out on a source audio file. Nowadays, off-line processing is accepted as a faster means of executing certain tasks.

Granular synthesis
A branch of synthesis that takes small 'granules' of sound which are then looped to create new sonic textures.

Buffer
A buffer is a temporary storage area in a device's RAM where sampled audio data is held.

Stylus RMX features Spectrasonics' new SAGE system for complete control over the tempo and feel of a drum loop. Note the corresponding MIDI file – this could be re-quantized to match the track.

recently the SAGE system (Spectrasonics Advanced Groove Engine), which is included in Stylus RMX.

Creatively speaking, beat slicing offers a much more creative approach to time manipulation by offering the possibility of re-arranging the MIDI triggers (Stylus RMX's Chaos Designer, for example, can automatically create variations within the loop to make the output less repetitive).

Moving beyond beat slicing, a growing number of programs and file formats offer an increasingly fluid approach to manipulating the tempo and pitch of an audio file. Apple Loops, Acidized .WAV files and Ableton's Live use a combination of slicing and granular time stretching to create truly elastic audio files that can be stretched to fit any pitch or tempo. For those new to recording, this kind of flexibility is often taken for granted, but it demonstrates how far pitch- and time-manipulation has come in the last few years.

Formant preservation

Even with the wonders of beat slicing and file formats such as Apple Loops, some old bugbears still remain – namely, munchkinisation on vocals. The identity of the human voice is contained in two chunks: the body and/or pitch of the note formed by the fundamental, and the formant peaks created in the upper harmonics. The exact positioning and frequencies of these formants are unique to each voice, as well as – more broadly speaking – the gender of a voice.

In the natural world, although a singer's fundamental frequency will change as they sing higher or lower in pitch, the formant peaks remain largely fixed. If the formants were to be shifted, the character and gender of the voice would change (possibly in extreme and unpleasant ways).

Traditional pitch-shifting techniques or varispeed will, of course, transpose all of the frequencies of the voice, shifting both the fundamental and the formants. This forced transposition is what we associate with munchkinisation, whereby the voice sounds unnaturally shifted (think Alvin And The Chipmunks).

Formant-preserving pitch shifting (as available on Roland's Variphrase system or Celemony's Melodyne 2) uses an advanced system that separates the formants from the main body of the sound. The results are suitably impressive; certainly much more natural than conventional pitch shifting.

If your plug-in enables specific processing of only the formants, some interesting gender transformation techniques can also be performed – without the need for surgery!

A stitch in time...

Although the automated time-and pitch-manipulation features offered by the likes of Ableton Live and Apple's GarageBand offer the quickest and most convenient means of stretching audio, there are many users who prefer a more detailed set of options to get a controllable result. Top-of-the-range products such as Serato's Pitch 'n Time, command a high price for both the quality and flexibility they offer, but their features enable users to explore both the creative and corrective aspects of this interesting field.

What's important, however, is remembering that although we have the means to fix almost any aspect of a recording, nothing beats the energy and vitality of a real, unmodified performance – even if it is a warts-and-all effort.

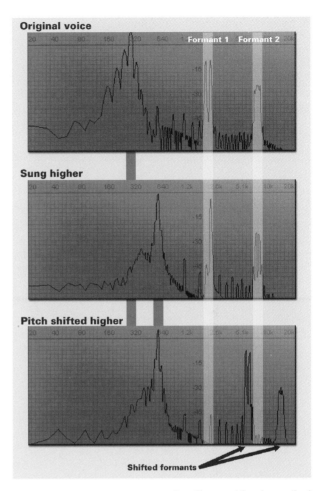

A vocal transposed through conventional pitch shifting will often display unnatural munchkinisation. Compare the different formant characteristics of a vocal sung at a higher pitch against the pitch-shifted original.

Further info

For more information on pitch shifting, formant preservation and an interesting article on pitch-correction techniques, visit:

www.eventide.com/technote/techn80.pdf
www.tc-helicon.tc/Files/helicon_files/Pitch_shifting.pdf
www.tc-helicon.tc/Default.asp?Id=2421

On a wider note, the following site contains some excellent tips and techniques on digital sound processing – especially in regard to time-based processing and transients.

http://mnorris.wellington.net.nz/soundmagic/tips.html

To find out more about some of the products mentioned in this article:

www.celemony.com
www.serato.com
www.eventide.com

Vocoders

Although the human voice is the most versatile and expressive of instruments, in true creative style musicians still like to change and modify it. A vocal that sounds in some way different to other vocals will stand out and attract attention to a recording.

One of the first commercial recordings to feature voice processing was Sparky's Magic Piano released by Capitol in 1947. This landmark children's story is still available today. It used a device called a Sonovox, which was mechanical in nature and worked by pressing two small disks to the performer's throat. Although it was not a vocoder and it worked in an entirely different way, the results were similar and many people assume the result was achieved with a vocoder.

The vocoder comes of age

The vocoder was developed in the 1930s by an employee of Bell Labs called Homer Dudley. Its original purpose was to improve speech transmission over telephone lines, essentially by reducing content to enable more data to be sent over the line's limited bandwidth. It was, in fact, also used during World War II to scramble telephone conversations between Franklin D Roosevelt and Winston Churchill.

The vocoder has been used in all forms of music – it was particularly prevalent in the pop and disco genres of the 70s – and regularly drops in and out of fashion. Memorable songs featuring a vocoder include Kraftwerk's We Are The Robots, Laurie Anderson's O Superman and ELO's Mr Blue Sky. The 1998 release of Cher's Believe heralded a new era of vocoder-processed tracks, the most renowned and recent of which being Madonna's American Life.

Initially, vocoders were only available as hardware devices. Some models from the early 1980s, such as the Korg VC-10 and Roland's VP-330 and SVC-350, were much in demand on the second-hand market when the analogue retro scene arrived in the 1990s, and some are still in use today. Modern hardware vocoders are still available (the Doepfer vocoder synth modules, for example) but the recent trend has been towards software plug-ins, which are often more versatile and, of course, much cheaper.

What's in a name?

It's not absolutely essential that you know exactly how a vocoder does its stuff in order to use one, but if you do know what's going on under the hood, you might find yourself using it in novel and unique ways.

The EMS Vocoder 2000 was one of the earliest commercially available vocoders.

Korg's VC-10, released in 1978, was used by Keith Emerson, Tomita, Rick Wakeman, Klaus Schulze and Tangerine Dream.

The name vocoder is derived either from VOice CODER, VOice enCODER or Voice Operated reCOrDER, depending on which source you read. A vocoder has two inputs called a carrier and a modulator, and if you're familiar with carrier and modulator terminology from FM synthesis you'll be way ahead of us. As the names suggest, the modulator modulates the carrier signal. In a vocoder, the modulator is usually a voice and the carrier is the signal that the modulation is imposed upon – usually a pad-type sound. This produces the typical 'talking synth' or 'robot voice' effect typically associated with vocoders.

Here's the techy explanation. A vocoder analyses the voice and splits it up into frequency bands, much like a spectral analyser. It might have six, eight, ten, twelve or more bands. Filters are also used to split the carrier signal into the same number of bands, each of which is controlled by a VCA (essentially it controls the volume of the frequency band in the carrier signal).

Let's assume you say something at a low pitch. This will be analysed into the lower bands, which in turn activate the lower-band VCAs, which will then pass the corresponding frequencies in the carrier signal. So when you talk, the analytical filters output energy levels corresponding to the frequencies in your voice with the result that the energy patterns of your voice are superimposed on the carrier.

It's not quite what you think

Note that it's the voice characteristics that are imposed upon the carrier, not the voice pitch, so to make your voice 'sing' you talk into the vocoder and generate the required notes by changing the pitch of the carrier, perhaps by playing a keyboard. When using a software vocoder, you'll probably pre-record the pitches you need for the carrier and then apply the vocal modulator to these.

The best carriers are those that are harmonically rich – so pads, strings and brass are good starting points. The carrier should contain the frequencies that are present in the vocal range being used. Our full vocal range runs from around 80Hz to 1kHz, although the range used in normal speech will be much less. The frequency range will also be different for men, women and children.

Tech terms

VCA

Voltage Controlled Amplifier. Typically, a synthesizer module that adjusts the volume of a signal according to its input. In a vocoder, the controlling signal is derived by analysing the frequencies in the modulator.

Voiced/unvoiced

The part of a vocoder that detects voiced (tonal) and unvoiced (noise) sections in a speech signal and makes the vocoder react accordingly.

Glide/slew

A control that smoothes the change between two discreet values. It's typically used in synthesizers to slide or glide between the pitches of two notes.

Note also that both sources are usually required in order to produce an output. If you stop talking or stop playing, the vocoder output will stop, too.

The power of software has meant that vocoders don't have to follow the format of their hardware predecessors and many feature far more controls. These may include an adjustable number of frequency bands (the more bands there are, the higher the definition of the audio), adjustable bandwidth (narrow bands will produce a thinner sound), filter and resonance controls, envelope settings (which determine how quickly the modulator triggers the carrier) and more besides.

The trouble with fricatives

Fricatives are high-pitched sounds, such as S, T, K, F and P, produced by the mouth rather than the vocal tract, and they often don't reproduce well on a vocoder. Some devices, therefore, add noise to duplicate the sound, while others use a low-pass filter to remove problem frequencies from the modulator. If your particular vocoder isn't playing ball, try compressing the vocal on the way into it, or compressing the audio track.

Pitch and carry

The range of effects you can generate with a vocoder is vast. Although naturally associated with voice effects, vocoders can be used with all sorts of sounds and, indeed, they can create many unique sounds suitable for a wide range of music. We won't go too far down the road of vocal processing here because we have a gargantuan Vocal Processing feature in next month's issue, so we'll round off this Ten Minute Master by suggesting ways of using a vocoder with mainly non-vocal sounds.

Drums are a firm favourite for vocoder processing. Run a drum loop through a vocoder using a pad for the carrier. Adjust the balance between the original signal and the modulated signal to determine how much of the processed sound you get. Adjust the filter settings so that it lets through more high frequencies to accentuate the hi-hats and mix these with the original sound. And try this way around – use a drum loop as the carrier and your voice as the modulator. Try speaking individual words and phrases, and then take a deep breath and roll out a whole load of words in one breath. Interesting…

We've already said that the carrier should match the modulator for frequency content and although most vocoders rely on a handful of tried-and-tested waveforms, it's worth experimenting with other carrier sounds such as wind, surf, rushing water, crowd noises and so on. Run a drum loop through this to produce a 'natural' drum sound.

Try reversing modulator and carrier signals. Knowing how vocoders work, you'll realise that a static modulator (such as a pad sound) will probably not produce interesting results. Dynamic natural sounds, on the other hand, may produce a few surprises…

Mix 'n' match

Not all vocoded effects have to be 'in yer face' – many intriguing and subtle effects can be created by mixing the processed signal with the original. Most

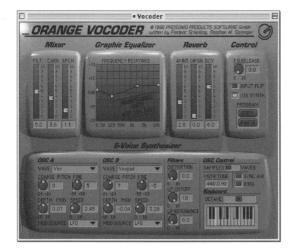

Although now showing its age to some extent, Prosoniq's Orange Vocoder plug-in is still one of the most popular software vocoder effects.

Most modern sequencing software includes vocoding functionality. This is Cubase VST's vocoder plug-in.

vocoders enable you to set the balance between the original and the modulated signal, but if you can't, it's easy enough to save the processed version, import it into your sequencer and adjust the balance in the mixer.

Try delaying the processed version a little to create a soft echo. Also, try panning the original and the processed signals to opposite sides of the stereo field. Take this a stage further by creating several copies of the processed signal, delay each one and place them at different pan positions to create a ghostly echo that pans around the stereo field.

You don't have to vocode every sound in a track. Here's an idea that may be best implemented on a drum track, but it will work with vocals and other tracks, too. From a track, cut out specific sounds and place them on their own track. On a drum track it could be the hi-hats or snare; with vocals it could be certain words or phrases. Now you can process just those parts of a sound. In many ways this can end up being more exciting than processing the entire track as the listener will be waiting for the section of music to come around that contains the 'strange' sound.

Try combining the last two techniques; create a processed version of individual drum hits or words, delay it a little and add it to the original to create a vocoded echo effect.

Vocoders are just about the most exciting, versatile and contemporary units for adding interest to your music, so experiment...

Further info

Wendy Carlos on vocoders
www.wendycarlos.com/vocoders.html
Other sources
www.vocoder-plugins.com
www.cim.mcgill.ca/~clark/nordmodularbook/nm_speech.html
www.lonestar.texas.net/~mr88cet/VocodingWebDemo/VocoderDemo.html
www.members.tripod.com/werdav/vocbaema.htm

Wireless systems

Like all things in the music technology industry, wireless systems have become much more affordable and prevalent, and are now available from a wide range of manufacturers, each system offering slightly different capabilities. Although not generally used within the studio environment, radio mics are regularly used for live music performances, in the theatre, and for television and film, providing freedom of movement and (potentially) invisible mic'ing techniques that are not possible with conventional microphones and cables.

FM transmission

The basic transmission principles of wireless systems are the same as conventional FM (frequency modulation) radio. A carrier wave defines the frequency at which the transmitter and receiver communicate. The amplitude of the audio source signal is used to modulate the frequency of the carrier wave and the result is transmitted as an electromagnetic wave. The receiver is tuned to the frequency of the carrier wave and demodulates it, re-creating the original audio input.

The frequency on which the transmitter and receiver both have to operate is analogous to a channel. When using more than one wireless system in close physical proximity, each system has to have its own dedicated channel and it is necessary to leave enough frequency 'space' between each of the systems. When using just two different wireless channels, a difference of 400kHz is usually sufficient, but when using multiple wireless systems (as is often the case now since in-ear monitoring became more popular), the frequencies of each channel have to be carefully selected to prevent intermodulation.

For radio microphones, the frequency of the carrier wave falls either within the VHF (very high frequency) or UHF (ultra high frequency) ranges. Both

With FM transmissions, the frequency of the carrier wave is modulated by the amplitude of the source audio.

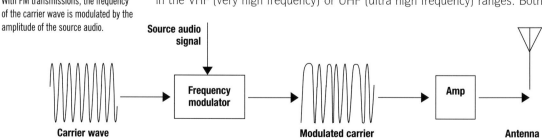

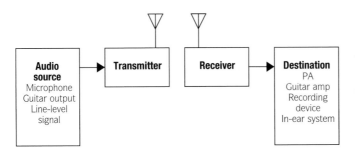

A wireless system comprises a receiver and transmitter, but each needs to be carefully selected to connect correctly to the source and destination.

VHF and UHF are within the MHz range (1MHz=1,000,000Hz); VHF covering 49–300MHz and UHF covering 300–1,000MHz.

The VHF range is very highly populated with traffic, as the cost of the equipment is significantly cheaper than for UHF. This popularity means that VHF wireless systems can be prone to interference from other radio signals – such as radio-controlled toys, walkie-talkies and conventional radio signals. This situation is exacerbated by the properties of VHF, as the carrier wave has a relatively longer wavelength and it can pass through a reasonable amount of non-metallic material. The result is that competing VHF signals are likely to be in the same space as your radio mic. The UHF carrier frequencies generally provide better performance, as these are less prone to external radio interference, give excellent line-of-sight reception and generally radiate only within the constraints of the venue.

Diversity

As UHF waves are radio (electromagnetic) waves, they display similar characteristics to sound waves and will reflect off surfaces within a room. This means that when using only a single-antenna receiver, it is possible that a reflected signal will arrive at the receiver at the same time as the direct signal and cause some phase cancellation, resulting in a partial (or total) signal drop-out.

Diversity reception solves this by using a pair of antennae to independently receive the same transmitted signal. The antennae are physically spaced apart from each other, the distance between the two being less than the wavelength of the carrier signal (for 900MHz the wavelength is approximately 33cm). This spatial difference means that phase cancellation is far less likely to occur at both antennae at the same time. With 'true diversity' systems, each antennae has an independent receiver and the signals are demodulated separately – the main unit continuously compares the signal strength from each and seamlessly switches to the strongest signal. Other diversity techniques involve combining the signal from the two independent receivers and building a stronger overall signal.

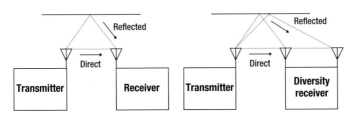

Two antennae of a diversity reception system can help reduce the chances of phase cancellation occurring.

Even medium-range wireless systems now offer UHF transmission and diversity reception.

Companding

The main principle with FM transmission is that the amplitude of the source audio signal modulates the frequency of the carrier wave: the wider the dynamic range of the source audio, the wider the resulting frequency variation of the carrier signal. As each carrier wave has a restricted bandwidth over which it is allowed to transmit, the dynamic range of the original audio has to be restricted.

FM radio signals have a dynamic range of only 40–50dB and this is the same for radio mics, so a technique called companding (or compansion) is used to maximise the dynamic range. This technique involves compressing the signal before transmission (generally using a ratio of around 2:1) and then performing a complementary expansion process (ratio of 1:2) once the received signal has been demodulated, restoring the original dynamic range.

Depending on the bandwidth allowed for the carrier signal, it is possible to achieve a 100dB dynamic range for the audio signal. Improved performance can be achieved by using multi-band compansion, whereby the original audio signal is split into two or more frequency bands and compressed and expanded individually.

The combination of compansion and the actual transmission processes can lead to an increase in high-frequency noise in the received signal. To counteract this, the original audio signal is 'pre-emphasised' before the compression stage. This pre-emphasis is a boosting of the higher frequencies that is equivalent to a 6dB/octave boost from around 4kHz upwards. After the expansion stage at the receiver, the signal is treated to an equivalent 'de-emphasis', resulting in a reduction in the high-frequency noise levels.

Compansion helps to expand the dynamic range of FM transmission using a combined process of compression and subsequent expansion.

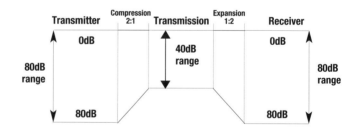

Squelch

Another major noise problem with radio mics occurs when the radio signal is lost at the receiver. As the receiver is searching for the carrier wave it can be prone to picking up background radio noise, which generally manifests itself as loud white noise. The Squelch control is a noise gate on the audio output of the receiver that is controlled by the strength of the received radio signal. When the radio signal drops below a threshold, the output of the receiver is silenced. This threshold level can be manually adjusted on the receiver and, as the radio transmission signal strength is distance-dependent, higher threshold levels will reduce the operating range of the radio mic, but will reduce the noise of the system.

A relatively recent refinement to the squelch system has been to use an inaudible 'key tone' (>25kHz) within the signal from the transmitter. The receiver still monitors the radio signal strength, but also continuously checks for the correct key tone, un-muting the audio output only when there is both the key tone and sufficient RF signal present.

Controlling the airwaves

The Joint Frequency Management Group (JMFG) regulates the frequencies used for radio microphone carrier waves in the UK. This body assigns the frequency bands within the UHF and VHF ranges for use with wireless systems. Even though these devices (should) use only localised transmission powers, they must not interfere with 'primary users' – TV and radio broadcasters, commercial communications or mobile phones.

Different groups within the frequency ranges allocated for radio microphones also exist: frequencies that do not require a licence; frequencies that require a licence and can be used anywhere in the UK; and frequencies that require a licence and are to be used in a specific location for a set period of time. Acquiring a licence – by approaching the JMFG – means access to a wider range of frequencies and less likelihood of localised interference.

A radio microphone may not replace a high-quality condenser mic in the studio, but wireless systems provide a vital function within the live performance environment and can, when appropriately used, increase your sense of freedom.

Further info

John Eargle's *The Microphone Book* 2nd Edition has a section dedicated to radio mics covering theoretical and practical aspects of radio mic use. Excellent resources on all aspects of wireless systems are at:
www.shure.com/booklets/wireless
www.audio-technica.com/cms/site/b1ef36f7cd249ff8/index.html
and the Joint Frequency Management Group:
www.jfmg.co.uk

Tech terms

Intermodulation
The interaction of radio signals and non-linear circuits to generate spurious signals that become part of the transmitted audio signal. It becomes a problem when the transmission of one radio system affects the performance of another. It can occur when using multiple wireless systems in very close proximity due to poor selection of the frequencies being used for each system.

Electromagnetic wave
A wave that travels at the speed of light and has both electrical and magnetic properties. An electromagnetic wave can travel through a vacuum.

In-ear monitoring
Foldback monitoring for live performance that is a wireless transmission to an earpiece worn by the performer.

Index

AAC, 30
active, 59
ADC, 48, 113
additive synthesis, 79
ADSR, 52
    envelope, 3
AIFF, 31
algorithms, 78
aliasing, 49
    frequencies, 45
amplitude, 87
analogue
    compressors, 33
    synthesis, 1
anechoic, 110
arranging, 7, 8
Attack, 32, 52
Attenuation, 57, 109
AU, 104, 107
audio analysis, 9
audio CDs
    software, 13
    burning, 13
    creating, 14
Audio Units, 104
audio,
    compressing, 27
    digital, 48
audio-to-digital converter, 48
automatic right, 39
auxiliary mix, 97

back-electret mics, 89
balanced, 19
balanced cables, 18
band pass, 58
    band-pass filters, 70
Band reject/Notch, 58
bandwidth, 57
bass, 6
Bass Manager, 130
beat slicing, 137
bi-directional, 90
bit, 113
breakpoint, 54, 79
breath control, 93
brick-wall limiter, 26
buffering, 30

buffer, 137
    buffer-underrun, 15
burning audio CDs, 13
busses, 97
butt splice, 67

cabling, 18
cardioid, 90, 123
carrier, 77
CD-R, 14, 17
CD-R drive, 13
CD-RW, 15, 17
checksum, 46, 47
clipping, 45, 50
codec, 30
codes, 16
coincident pair, 121
companding, 146
compression, 23, 32
    audio, 27
    look-ahead, 26
    lossy, 30
    optical, 24
    soft-knee, 26
compressors, 33
condenser microphone, 89, 97, 123
connections
    balanced, 19
    unbalanced, 19
connectors, XLR, 19
continuous controller message, 93
contour generator, 52
Copyright Act, 38
copyright, 36
    Copyright Act, 38
    The UK Copyright Service, 37
    US Copyright Office, 38
corrupt data, 46
CPU, 107
CRC codes, 46
crossfades, 64
cutoff frequency, 56
cutoff point, 56
cycle ratio, 82
cyclic redundancy checks, 46

DAC, 48, 113
damping attenuation, 109

data, corrupt, 46
dBFS, 130
DDL, 42
decay, 52, 110
decay time, 109
decibel, 50
delay, 40, 110
    multi-tap, 111
delay time, 110
density, 109
diffusion, 109
digital audio, 48
    compressors, 33
    converter, 48
    delay lines, 42
    digital bit overflow distortion, 45
    digital-to-audio converter, 48
    errors, 44
    mixers, 98
digital video, 72
digitising audio, 48
directional response mic, 90
disc at once, 13
distortion, 45
    intermodulate, 62
dithering, 45
diversity, 145
download, 27
drive parameter, 62
drop-frame dips, 134
drum, 6
    drum score, 8
    kick, 7
DSP, 107
    DSP cards, 106
DX, 107
DX7, 77
DXi, 107
dynamic equalisation, 63
dynamic mics, 88
dynamic range, 50

early reflections, 109
electromagnetic wave, 147
envelopes, 52
    rate/level, 77
    envelope generator, 52
EQ, 56
    fixed, 57
    graphic, 58
    parametric, 58
    sweeping/semi-parametric, 58
equalisation, 56
    dynamic, 63
exciters, 60
expression, 93

fade-in, 65
fades, 64
Fast Fourier Transform, 10
feedback, 110
FFT, 10
    analysis, 10
    waterfalls, 10

figure-of-8, 90
    figure-of-8 mic, 122
filters, 68
    active, 59
    FIR, 47
    passive, 59
    types, 58
FIR filters, 47
FireWire, 72
    FireWire 400, 73
    FireWire 800, 73
fixed EQ, 57
FM synthesis, 75
FM transmission, 144
formant, 71
    preservation, 138
Fourier Analysis, 9
frame, 17
    frame rates, 135
frequency, 84, 86
    aliasing frequencies, 45
    attenuation, 109
    domain, 12
    frequency divider, 3, 4
    response, 56
    sample, 45
fundamental, 56

gain, 32, 57
gate pulse, 3
gates, 3
General MIDI, 94
glide/portamento, 4
glide/slew, 142
glitch, 67
grain cloud, 82
grain size, 80
grain spacing, 80
granular synthesis, 80, 83, 137
graphic EQ, 58
graphs, 10
ground, 22
growl, 56

hard-knee compression, 26
harmonics, 71, 84
    pulse, 102
    saw, 101
    sine, 101
    square, 102
    triangle, 101
harmonics and partials, 86
harmonic number, 85, 101, 102
harmonic series, 85
headroom, 50
hertz, 103
high pass, 58
high shelf, 59
high-pass filter, 70
HTDM, 107
hypercardioid, 90, 123

iLink, 73
index points, 17

indices, 17
in-ear monitoring, 147
input section, 96
insert point, 99
interference, 22
interleaving, 46
intermodulate distortion, 62
intermodulation, 147
IPS, 43

jacks, 19
jitter, 46

key mapping, 113
key splitting, 115
keyboards, 6
kick drum, 7

layering, 115
legato, 126
level, 57
LFE, 130
LFO, 3
license, 39
Lissajous, 10, 11
longitudinal time code, 133
look-ahead compression, 26
loom, 22
loop points, 113
lossy compression, 30
low frequency oscillator, 3
low pass, 58
low shelf, 59
low-pass filter, 70
LTC, 132, 133

machine control, 134
mark/space ratio, 102
MAS, 107
master section, 96
MCPS, 37
Mellotron, 124
microphones, 88
    back-electret, 89
    bi-directional, 90
    condenser mics, 89, 97, 123
    directional response, 90
    dynamic mics, 88
    figure-of-8, 122
    omni-directional, 90
    radio, 144
    ribbon, 90
    shotgun, 90
    soundfield, 122
    tube, 90
middle and side, 12, 122
MIDI, 92
    General MIDI, 94
MIDI clock, 132
MIDI Implementation Chart, 93
MIDI In, 94
MIDI Machine Control, 134
MIDI Out, 94
MIDI Thru, 94

MIDI Thru box, 94
MIDI time code, 133
mix, 62, 109
    auxiliary, 97
mix/balance, 110
mixdown, 7
mixers, 96
    digital, 98
mLAN, 75
MMC, 134
modulation wheel, 93
modulator, 103
modules, 2
monitor section, 96
mono jack, 19
Moog, 1
moral right, 39
MP3, 27, 31
MPEG Audio Layer 3, 27
MPEG4, 30
MTC, 132, 133
multi-sampling, 114
multi-session, 14
multi-tap, 42
    multi-tap delay, 111
Musical Instrument Digital Interface, 92

near-coincident pair, 121
notch filters, 70
note off message, 93
note on message, 93
Nyquist limit, 49
Nyquist's Theorem, 45

off-line processing, 137
Ogg Vorbis, 30
omni-directional, 90
operators, 78
optical compression, 24
oscillators, 100
overburning, 16
oversampling, 45, 49

pad, 97
pan, 93, 98
paragraphic EQ, 58
parameters, 16
parametric EQ, 58
parity bit, 47
partials, 79, 86
passive, 59
patchbay, 21, 98
pattern-based sequencers, 117
phantom power, 91, 97
phase cancellation, 43
pickup pattern, 90
ping-pong, 42
    delay, 110
piracy, 36
pitch, 136
    shifting, 113, 137
pizzicato, 126
plug-ins, 104
polar pattern, 123

poles, 57
post-fade, 99
preamp, 91
pre-fade, 99
pre-fader, 97
Pro Tools, 105
program change message, 93
proximity effect, 91
pulse   harmonics, 102
    waves, 100
    width, 102
pumping, 35

Q, 57
quantizing distortion, 45
QuickTime, 31

radio microphones, 144
RAM, 113
rate/level envelopes, 77
RealAudio, 30
Red Book, 13
release, 32, 52, 53
resolution, 50
resonance, 57
reverb, 108, 110
reverberation, 110
rhythm, 5
rhythm section, 8
ribbon mics, 90
ring modulator, 4
ripping, 30
rolloff, 57
room simulators, 109
RT60, 110
RTAS, 107
run-in/run-out blocks, 17

S/PDIF, 134
sample and hold, 4
samplers, 112, 124
    multi-sampling, 114
    sample frequency, 45
    sample rate, 48, 112
    sample resolution, 50, 112
saturate distortion, 45
saw harmonics, 101
sawtooth wave, 100
sequencers, 116
    pattern-based, 117
shotgun, 90
side chain, 35
signal-to-noise ratio, 50
sine harmonics, 101
sine wave, 84, 100
slapback, 41
slew limiter, 4
slope, 57
slur, 4
SMPTE timecode, 133
SMPTE/EBU, 133
soft and hard knee, 26, 35
soft-knee compression, 26
software compressors, 33

song position pointer, 132
sonogram, 10
soundfield microphones, 122
space echoes, 41
spaced pair, 121
spectral analysis, 71
spectrogram, 10
spectrographs, 10
spiccato, 126
SPP, 132
square harmonics, 102
square wave, 100
squelch, 146
stacking, 115
stage box, 22
step entry, 117
stereo, 120
stereo jack, 19
stream, 27
string machines, 124
string synths, 124
striping, 133, 134
(sub)group section, 96
sub-harmonics, 63
sub-oscillator, 3
subtractive synthesis, 4, 68
surround sound, 128
sustain, 52, 53
sweeping/semi-parametric EQ, 58
sync track, 134
synchronisation, 132
synthesis, 1
    additive, 79
    FM, 76
    granular, 80, 83, 137
    subtractive, 68
    wavetable, 82

tape delay systems, 41
taps, 43
TDIF, 134
TDM, 107

Theremin, 1
threshold, 32
timbre, 87, 113
time, 136
    domain, 12
    stretching, 137
timecode, 132
    SMPTE, 133
track at once, 13
transients, 62, 63
    transient generator, 52
transition, 67
tremolo, 4, 126
triangle harmonics, 101
triangle wave, 100
triggers, 3
TRS jacks, 19
tube mics, 90
tune parameter, 62

UHF, 145

UK Copyright Service, 37
unbalanced, 19
US Copyright Office, 38
USB 1/1, 73
USB 2.0, 73

variable bit rate, 29
varispeed, 136
VCA, 2, 142
VCF, 2
VCO, 2
velocity crossfading, 115
velocity switching, 114
vertical interval time code, 133
VHF, 145
vibrato, 4
VITC, 132, 133
vocoders, 140
voiced/unvoiced, 142
voltage control, 2
voltage controlled amplifier, 2
voltage controlled filter, 2
voltage controlled oscillator, 2

volume, 93
volume shaping, 52
VST, 104, 107
VST Instruments, 104
VSTi, 107

waterfalls, 10
WAV, 31
wavetable synthesis, 82
wet and dry, 110
wha, 56
white noise, 79
width, 109
Windows Media, 30
wireless systems, 144

XLR connectors, 19

zero-crossing point, 66, 82
zones, 115
Z-plane, 71

5.1 surround sound, 128